SOUL SOOTHERS
Mini Meditations For Busy Lives

CINDY GRIFFITH-BENNETT

FINDHORN PRESS

Published in 2013 by Findhorn Press, Scotland

ISBN 978-1-84409-608-4

A CIP record for this title is available from the British Library.

Edited by Michael Hawkins
Cover design and illustrations by Richard Crookes
Interior design by Damian Keenan
Printed and bound in the EU

1 2 3 4 5 6 7 8 9 17 16 15 14 13

Published by
Findhorn Press
117-121 High Street,
Forres IV36 1AB,
Scotland, UK

t +44 (0)1309 690582
f +44 (0)131 777 2711
e info@findhornpress.com
www.findhornpress.com

Contents

Acknowledgments 10

1. Why Meditate? 12

2. Where and When Can I Meditate? 19

3. The Twenty-Second Meditation 24
   The Twenty-Second Meditation 24
      Where and When 25
      Example 26
      Why – The Need for Quiet Time 26
      Soul Soother 27

4. The Breathing Meditations 28
   The Breathing Meditation – Sensing the Air 28
   The Breathing Meditation – Counting 29
   The Breathing Meditation – Counting When Sitting Down 29
      Where and When 30
      Example 30
      Why – The Importance of Breath 31
      Soul Soother 32

5. The Grounding Meditations 34
   The Grounding Meditation – Roots 34
   The Grounding Meditation – Red Cord 35
      Where and When 36
      Example 37
      Why – The Benefits of Grounding 37
      Soul Soother 41

6. The Staying-in-Your-Energy Meditation 43

The Staying-in-Your-Energy Meditation 43

    Where and When 44

    Example 45

    Why – Energetic Exchange Between People 47

    Soul Soother 53

7. The Walking Meditations 54

The Walking Meditation – Sensation 54

The Walking Meditation – Adding the Breath 55

The Walking Meditation – Enjoying Nature 56

    Where and When 57

    Example 57

    Why – Mindfulness 58

    Soul Soother 60

8. The Bell Meditation 62

The Bell Meditation 62

    Where and When 63

    Example 64

    Why – Discernment vs. Judgment 64

    Soul Soother 66

9. The Blessing Meditations 68

The Blessing Meditation – For People 68

The Blessing Meditation – For Situations in the Future 69

The Blessing Meditation – For Situations in the Present Moment ... 70

    Where and When 71

    Example 72

    Why – Gratitude Is the Attitude 73

    Soul Soother 75

10. The Review Meditation 76

The Review Meditation – Lunchtime 76

Where and When 77

Example 78

Why – Karma and Service 78

Soul Soother 82

11. The Activity Meditation 83

The Washing Dishes Meditation 83

Where and When 84

Example 84

Why – Intuition 85

Soul Soother 88

12. The Noise Meditation 90

The Noise Meditation 90

Where and When 91

Example 92

Why – The Vibration Effect 92

Soul Soother 97

13. The Observation Meditation 98

The Observation Meditation 98

Where and When 99

Example 100

Why – Interconnection 101

Soul Soother 103

14. The Mantra Meditation 105

The Mantra Meditation 105

Where and When 106

Example 107

Why – The Power of Sound and Word 107

Soul Soother 110

15. The Contemplation Meditation 111

The Three-Minute Contemplation Meditation 111

Where and When 112

Example 113

Why – Contemplation 114

Soul Soother 115

16. The Attitude Adjuster Meditation 117

The Attitude Adjuster Meditation 117

Where and When 118

Example 119

Why – Universal Law of Polarity 120

Soul Soother 121

17. The Chakra Meditations 122

The Chakra Meditation – Healing Color 122

The Chakra Meditation – Balancing the Chakras 123

Where and When 124

Example 125

Why – Chakras within the Physical Body 126

The Seven Main Chakras 130

Soul Soother 135

18.

The Golden Light Meditation 137

The Golden Light Meditation 137

Where and When 139

Example 139

Why – Chakras Outside the Physical Body 140

Soul Soother 144

19. The Outer Bodies Meditation 146

The Outer Bodies Meditation 146

Where and When 147

Example 148

Why – The Outer Bodies 149

Soul Soother 155

20. The Light Work Meditation 157

The Light Work – Space Clearing Meditation 157

Where and When 158

Example 159

Why – Using Light Work 159

Soul Soother 162

Conclusion 163

Endnotes 171

Bibliography 172

About the Author 173

Acknowledgments

*S*oul Soothers: Mini Meditations for Busy Lives came from my students over the last twenty years asking for a way to bring peace, calm, mindfulness, and spiritual growth into their lives without sacrificing family, job, and all the responsibilities life piles up on them. So first, I must thank my students.

I would never have seen myself as an author if Pam Liflander had not seen my potential over 12 years ago. Thank you Pam for all your support and assistance, it has been a long road. I was lucky enough to have met Sabine, Thierry, Gail, and the rest of the amazing Findhorn Press group through their publishing of David's and my book, *Voyage of Purpose*. They have been so supportive of my vision for Soul Soothers, put up with me asking a million questions, making a dozen suggestions, and always making me feel they value my thoughts. David and I hope someday to get to Findhorn and meet you all in person.

When I wasn't sure how to word something or the proper way to punctuate, Pax Vlietstra was always an email away. So when you read something particularly well worded, it might very well be Pax's words, not mine. Erin Clermont took my rough manuscript, and through her wonderful editing, helped me sound like a grown up writer, teaching me to eliminate the word *that* from my vocabulary. I also want to thank my nephew, Jon Hansen who helped with my vibrational theory to make sure my wave diagrams were right.

I would never have gotten *Soul Soothers* written if it wasn't for Creekside Books and Café in my hometown of Skaneateles NY. Thank you Erika, and the rest of the group, for bearing with me as we finally figured out the perfect way to prepare my decaf ice tea and for letting me sit there for hours and hours, day after day!

My Mother, Mary-Gray Griffith, once gave all us girls a little pamphlet with her words of wisdom. Most were common sense motherly things like *Use moisturizer every day.* Yet one thing she said always stayed with me: *Just believe in something.* With those four words, my mother gave me permission to be free of the limitations of my society, my peers, and even my religious upbringing. Those four words allowed me to believe in my path and myself. My mother has always supported me 100% in anything that I have attempted (I remember when first starting as a psychic, she bought a silk pouch for my Tarot Cards). Words cannot express how much her support has meant to me over the years. Thank you, Mother and my whole family for all the encouragement you have offered David and me as we embark on our literary adventures.

My friends have listened to me go on and on about this book, reassuring me when I felt overwhelmed, so thank you Kiki, Anne, and Lesley. Most of all, I want to thank my husband, David Bennett. Thank you for being a strong, steady pillar as I whirled around you like a crazy person. You have no idea how much you inspire me everyday to be the best person I can. Thank you for doing all the quotes for Soul Soothers, being my technology guru, and for being my best friend. I love you deeply.

Finally, thank you all for taking the time out of your busy life to read *Soul Soothers.* I hope you come to see the potential you all have to become positive and empowering individuals who can truly make a difference in this world by raising your vibration and sharing your light, and please, always believe in something.

Thank you,
Cindy Griffith-Bennett

CHAPTER 1

Why Meditate?

Meditating should be a relief not a labor.
We are able to center our concentration in simple ways.
— *DAVID BENNETT, Voyage of Purpose*

If you're reading a book on meditation, you may already appreciate the benefits of a meditation practice. Meditation and its accompanying relaxation have been shown to physically decrease pulse rate, blood pressure, respiration rate, oxygen consumption, and muscle tension. Mentally, it produces an alpha brain wave and heightened cognitive ability.[1] Spiritually, relaxation and meditation are the keys to opening up to your higher guidance.

Yet the other reason you might be reading this particular book is because you have no idea how to add one more thing into your already packed life. *Soul Soothers: Mini Meditations for Busy Lives* helps you to fit meditation into your day — without sacrificing precious time with the children, job, mate, parent, or any of the other "must do's" on your schedule.

Soul Soothers is designed for busy people like you, whose life is strong on achievement yet lacking in tranquility. It offers ways to add peaceful and calming moments into your hectic life without the guilt that accompanies taking too much "me" time.

"Me" time is hard to find, even if you choose not to feel guilty about it! In the chapters to come, you will find meditations that are specifically designed to take advantage of moments in your existing daily routine that can be turned into meditation and relaxation opportunities. These meditations can be used just as easily while standing in the grocery line as sitting on a meditation cushion at the spa. Most of us do not have spa time on our agenda this week, yet waiting in line is inevitable. These meditations offer you relaxation in under a minute and can be expanded for even greater relaxation when you have more time. You will also find a few meditations that can be done as you go to sleep, helping you to relax, sleep deeply, and prepare for tomorrow's demands.

The majority of the meditations presented in this book concern mindfulness, or focus. They help you to relax and de-stress, as you develop focus and awareness. Picture your mind as one of those flashlights that you can twist one way so that the light becomes brighter, stronger, and concentrated and turn the other way to scatter the light to cover a larger area. Meditation takes a mind that is scattered (the flashlight when it is set to spread out) and through focus makes thoughts more concentrated — and therefore more powerful (like the flashlight on the most concentrated setting). When your thoughts are focused and concentrated, you think more clearly and are more productive with your time.

Focused and Concentrated   Unfocused and Scattered

Meditation as a form of mindfulness practice has been proven to increase focus, lessen stress, strengthen memory, lower blood pressure, improve sleep, and promote stronger intuition. A recent study was performed over four days with one group doing mindfulness training and another group listening to an audio book. Both groups had a general mood improvement, yet only the participants using the short-term mindfulness training experienced reduced fatigue, less anxiety, and increased mindfulness. Plus they significantly improved working memory and executive functioning. The research findings suggest that even short-term practice can provide benefits that have previously been reported by long-term meditators.[2] This tells us that we can obtain many of the health and spiritual benefits of meditation from shorter practices.

Spiritual growth is another reason you may have decided to practice meditation. Each chapter of *Soul Soothers* includes the spiritual benefits of the meditation as well as a short lesson on a related spiritual topic. Meditation has long been taught as one of, if not the most important tool for spiritual growth. Your soul will thank you for adding meditation to your day. While you are gaining physical and mental benefits, meditation will also assist you in training your mind to allow your soul's wisdom to be heard. Your soul is an important part of your daily life. You probably don't think about your soul when making your to-do list. Yet your soul contains all you need to know in order to make the most of the time you have here on earth. Life goes quickly and your soul isn't going to wait until you have the time to do nothing but contemplate your navel. Who has that kind of time?

Your soul is in constant interaction with you, helping you to be patient and kind as well as assisting you when it is time to stand up for yourself. Think of your soul as having an encyclopedia that contains all you need to be the best parent, teacher, child, lover, coworker, and good person in general. Your guides and angels are also available for help. Think of guides as having written the encyclopedia. You have worked with your guides in planning this lifetime and they are there, along with the angels, to assist you in making the most of your time on Earth. When you gain even the smallest amount of control of your mind through meditation, your soul, guides, and angels can start to download helpful information for you to use. Your guidance may come through a thought, hunch, idea, or even a synchronistic event, when two connected events happen together even though it is unlikely they would. A synchronistic event, demonstrating your guides working with you, could be when you need to contact a person and that person calls you. Be assured, your soul and other higher guidance is in constant contact with you, supplying the help you need. The best way to achieve this clearer communication is through developing stronger focus through mindfulness, deeper relaxation, and keener intuition. Meditation offers you all of that.

As you continue to get comfortable with focus and mindfulness meditations, your ability to connect with your guides' and angels' higher guidance will increase. Accessing your higher guidance will allow you to recognize the opportunities your soul, guides, and angels are presenting to you for growth and service during the day, in a way that you can evolve and still pick up the kids on time!

Shorter meditation time is the key to *Soul Soothers*. You will learn how to turn simple chores like washing dishes and taking a shower into meditations. You will find that walking from your desk to the meeting will never be the same after experiencing the benefits of the Walking Meditation. The Mantra Meditation will help change your focus from work to home without taking more time than turning on the car. All of these meditation opportunities are a part of your life already, yet you will begin to see them as perfect occasions to enjoy the calming effect of practicing meditation throughout your day. When you are in bed and your mind is keeping you up, unable to stop processing your day, the Review Meditation will assist you in going through your day without judging and obsessing. You'll find the best way to handle the situation if it comes up again and then be able to let it go. Or you can choose the Chakra Balancing Meditation, which will quiet your mind at bedtime and strengthen your Energetic System, making you healthier and less likely to catch your co-worker's cold!

Many people have misconceptions about meditation and these can sabotage your ability to enjoy the benefits of it. The biggest misconception is that you "should" be able to clear your mind. "Should" is one of the chief stress-creating words in the dictionary. There is no "should" in this type of meditation, and you are not expected to clear your mind. What you *will* do is find you're getting better at ignoring the thoughts that come through during your meditation. For example, think of your thoughts like TV commercials. You know you don't have to pay attention to them and you're bound to come across them again. You can hear them without listening to them. In meditation, your stray thoughts are treated the same way. You know the thoughts are playing, you can acknowledge them, but you don't have to focus your attention on them or let them frustrate you. Another advantage of the meditations in this book is that they are short, which means you are less likely to have thoughts sidetrack you.

Another misconception is that you "should not" be frustrated by meditation. Even with these short meditations, you may be compelled to admit how hard it is for your mind to focus where you want it. This will undoubtedly frustrate you! But don't worry; this is normal at the beginning. Since poor focus is likely one reason why you decided to meditate, you can feel better knowing you are going to improve. So, release any expectations you might have. In first attempts at meditation your mind is like a little child. It doesn't want to be controlled and its attention span is miniscule. Little by little, you will find your ability to meditate growing. Like a child, it takes time for the mind to adjust to each level of growth. At first, just laugh at your mind's immaturity.

Laughter is a meditation in itself. The more serious you try to be with these meditations the harder it will be to use them. This book is designed to bring peace and calm into your day, not create more places in which to judge yourself. Most likely, you will not get it right the first time or the second time. Getting it right isn't the objective. Feeling relaxed and ready for your day by offering yourself a healthy "time-out" is the goal!

Time-outs are often used as a children's discipline measure, but at core they are a tool to help the child think about what has just happened. Time-outs bring mindfulness into our life — and they are not only for misbehavior. The benefit of mindfulness is not the only thing you will learn as you read about each meditation. Each chapter is designed to help you understand the "Why" of the meditation you are doing. Besides mindfulness, you will learn about the power of breath, the benefits of grounding, how energy is exchanged, how to deal with unhealthy people and situations, discernment versus judgment, the real deal on karma, how gratitude improves your day, all about the Chakras and the Outer Bodies, how you are interconnected to everything, the benefits of contemplation, opening yourself to your intuition, how vibrations and sound affect you, and why Light Work is such a powerful tool.

Each chapter can be used as a class, teaching you one type of meditation, explaining where and when to use it and showing you a "how it works" example. The example is specifically designed to demonstrate how you can tweak the meditation to fit your situation. This is followed by the spiritual lesson behind the meditation that soothes the soul. This "where, when, why, and Soul Soother" format allows you to practice one meditation until you are ready for another, look at all the meditations and pick out which you like best, or decide what spiritual lesson you want to learn and practice the corresponding meditation. Either way, these meditations are designed for busy people like you with real lives. If you don't want to read the whole book at once, use the Table of Contents, which provides a breakdown of each meditation name, page number, and what you will learn from it.

No matter how you use *Soul Soothers*, this is an opportunity for you to bring greater peace, tranquility, and intuition into your busy schedule without the time and guilt associated with a structured daily meditation practice. Read on to learn about the many opportunities in your daily life that are ready and waiting to be filled with blissful serenity.

CHAPTER 2

Where and When Can I Meditate?

Know there are are messages all around us, in the
whispers of the leaves, the call of a dove, an unexpected
rainbow, Love is everywhere.
Keeping focused and steady with Love in our heart,
sustains us in the universal flow, so we may relate and
contribute loving intentions to others.

- *DAVID BENNETT, Voyage of Purpose*

You can basically meditate anywhere. Yet being realistic, when and where best depends on the meditation. In *Soul Soothers*, you'll find meditations specifically designed to be accomplished without changing your routine. For example, the Activity Meditation turns two minutes of your shower, which you have to do anyway, into a meditation that leaves you focused. If you add a minute or two of Golden Light Meditation to the same shower, you will clear your Energetic System and set up an aura of loving vibration that will be felt by all you come in contact with. So, instead of spending your shower dreading your upcoming day at work, you'll do four minutes of meditation — and gain benefits that will accompany you throughout your day. It sounds too good too be true, but researchers have shown how even short meditations have real, positive affects on your memory and executive function such as planning, working memory, attention, problem solving, verbal reasoning, mental flexibility, and multitasking.[3] These results can be achieved by adding short meditations, like the meditations presented in *Soul Soothers,* to your day.

The Breathing and Grounding Meditations can be practiced as you sit at your desk or prepare your child's cereal. These two meditations, along with others you'll find in this book, do not require you to close your eyes or even stop what you are doing. Everyone has to breathe, so the only difference people might notice when you're practicing one of the Breath Meditations is that you look more relaxed!

Another meditation, specifically designed to assist you when you are around unhealthy situations or people, helps you to briefly disengage so that you can collect your thoughts and avoid getting caught up in the drama of the situation, without having to run away. The Walking Meditation creates a sacred space for you anywhere you have to walk, which is just about everywhere. Even a trip to the restroom can provide the mindfulness break you need to review what your priorities are and what might be taking you off track. Figuring you have to walk to your car, the restroom, and lunch, you can easily add at least five minutes of meditation to the four you had to start the day off. You are now up to nine minutes of meditation today!

Learning how to turn everyday sounds into the Bell Meditation offers five or six opportunities to stop and take a few seconds to re-center. The Blessing Meditation adds short bursts of sacred time into your schedule. I like to use the Blessing Meditation every time I say hello to someone. So, with these two, very short meditation opportunities, you could add another three minutes of meditation, bringing your total to twelve minutes of serenity in your busy day.

The Review Meditation is perfect for right after you finish your lunch or before you begin an important conversation. This meditation allows you to go over your past action and choose whether you want to repeat it or come up with a better way to handle the situation. It allows you to be discerning about your actions without judging yourself. "I love myself and will do better next time," is the mantra of this meditation. If you wish to do a formal Mantra Meditation, you can take thirty seconds to repeat a word or phrase in order to create the desired mindset. The Mantra Meditation can be practiced anytime you need to break up obsessive thoughts or create a pause from what you were doing and what you are about to do. Being that I am a psychic, it is easy to keep thinking about my work after I have finished. I like to use the Mantra Meditation when I am finished with a client in order to end that part of my life and go on with my private life. My students like to do the Mantra Meditation after they are done with work or if they are about to say something they think they might regret. Putting these two meditations into your day, you have added another five minutes. You have now gone over the fifteen minutes of meditation that is recommended for beginners — and you haven't even gone grocery shopping yet!

Grocery shopping is a wonderful time to do an Observation Meditation. Watching the grocery checkout line each time you stand in an aisle doesn't slow down your shopping, rather it gives you an opportunity to observe how people go about choosing which lane they want. Are the majority mindless shoppers, who simply go to the first line they see, or are they picky line choosers who look at all the lines and size of people's carts before they make their choice? The Observation Meditation helps you to realize your interconnection with others and your surroundings, and how your environment, and the people in it, affects your choices and energy. You can add another few minutes of meditation to your shopping by practicing the Attitude Adjuster Meditation as you wait in the checkout line. Has the shopping relaxed you or stressed you out? Look at how you feel, imagine how you want to feel, and use the Attitude Adjuster Meditation to help get yourself in your desired headspace. During shopping you have now added another four minutes to your meditation total and still have not had to put your day on hold!

The Contemplation Meditation in *Soul Soothers* uses a three-minute hourglass egg timer, yet you can use the same technique while cooking pasta. As the water boils, concentrate only on the boiling water. Then allow your mind to ponder a problem you have. Being aware of when your mind wanders, bring it back to the water boiling and then start to contemplate again. While making dinner you have added another three minutes to your meditation total, gotten some clarity on your problem, and did not overcook the pasta.

The Grounding Meditation can be used anytime you feel clumsy or less than on the ball. It is also perfect for re-centering after the kids have gone off to bed or when you have finished your nightly chores. Grounding takes less than a minute, yet the results can last all day.

The last three meditations in *Soul Soothers*, the Light Work Meditation for Clearing Space, the Chakra Meditation, and the Outer Bodies Meditation, are best saved for when you won't be interrupted. Most people would not use all three of these meditations on a daily basis, yet choosing one offers another five or ten minutes of meditation first thing in the morning before you get out of bed, last thing before you go to sleep, or some point in between if you can squeak out the time. You can shorten any of these meditations and be done in less than a minute, yet they are so relaxing and soothing that you might want to allow yourself the extra few minutes.

Without taking any time away from your already hectic schedule, you have added about a half hour of meditation to your day without having to go behind closed doors, sit cross-legged on a cushion, or light incense. Those are wonderful options if you have the time and any of the meditations you have learned here can be lengthened and enjoyed with incense if you choose. Yet it is nice to know that you won't have to hide away to gain the benefits of meditation or sacrifice any part of your full day. Starting with the Twenty-Second Meditation in the next chapter will allow you to begin meditating right away!

CHAPTER 3

The Twenty-Second Meditation

It is so important we not be so overwhelmed with living in this physical world, that we forget to spend time in silence, getting to know our vital life force that makes up our being that will live forever.

— *DAVID BENNETT, Voyage of Purpose*

The Twenty-Second Meditation

1. If possible, support your elbows on a table or your lap.
2. Take three deep breaths, and with each exhalation, feel your shoulders relaxing.
3. Return to your regular breathing.
   Place your head in your hands, with your hands fully supporting your head.
4. Bring your attention to the weight of your head on your hands. Simply be aware of that weight for a few moments and let go of everything else in your world.
5. Gently close your eyes, keeping the distractions to a minimum.
6. Acknowledge and release any thoughts other than your head in your hands. Return your focus to the weight of your head in your hands.
7. Breathe in and out normally, feel your breath on your hands. Release all your stress and tension as you exhale.

8. Inhale strength and energy, while you once again exhale your stress.
9. Feeling your head totally supported by your hands, allow your neck and shoulders to let go of the responsibility of carrying the weight of your head. Permit yourself the feeling of being totally supported by your hands.
10. Bring your attention back to the weight of your head in your hands. When all of your focus is on the weight of your head in your hands and you feel relaxed, feel your feet on the ground, and gently lift your head.
11. Open your eyes and observe how clear-minded you feel. Now return to your task.

WHERE AND WHEN

Here is a meditation you can use at work, whenever you need a quick break, or simply do not have a lot of time. This simple method can help you center your thoughts and become more efficient with work or anything else you are doing. The Twenty-Second Meditation is best done at a desk or someplace where you can support your elbows. If you don't have a place to do it comfortably, try the restroom. (Whereby, it is also called the Potty Meditation.) You could also use the Twenty-Second Meditation in a waiting room, the car before you start to drive, or upon arriving home. It is also perfect for telling your mind that it is time to go to sleep, by simply taking twenty seconds as you sit on the side of the bed! Need to clear your head before talking to your boss, parent's nurse, or child's teacher? Take twenty seconds out before your conversation and you'll find yourself ready, focused, and clear!

EXAMPLE

Eliza is about to give a presentation to a group of very important clients. She has been rushing all day to get the PowerPoint just right. She has about five minutes to get to the conference room, just enough time for a quick stop. Eliza pops into the restroom, takes a seat, and rests her head in her hands. She takes twenty seconds, feeling all of the tension drain out of her neck as she allows her hands to take on the weight of her head. As she finishes up her meditation, Eliza feels refocused and supported. Giving herself a smile in the mirror, Eliza heads down the hall to her very successful presentation!

WHY - THE NEED FOR QUIET TIME

The Twenty-Second Meditation works for a number of reasons. First, you only need to find twenty seconds to stop and refocus. Also, you now have twenty seconds in which you actually feel supported during your day. Life goes by so quickly that it is easy to forget to take the time to refill your cup by taking care of yourself and surrounding yourself with supportive people. Going from one situation to the next, when it seems everyone wants something from you, use the Twenty-Second Meditation to create a space for you to do nothing other than feel supported! This meditation also reminds you to release the tension in your neck and shoulders. Often by the end of the day, many people have put all their stress in their upper back and wonder why they can't relax when it is time to fall asleep. Take twenty seconds out of your day, and when you see how easy this meditation is, you might choose it other than times when you are stressed. Allowing yourself to release tension and bring focus and support into your life avoids taking even more time out of your day for a visit to the chiropractor!

SOUL SOOTHER

Your soul will thank you every time you allow yourself even a few moments of quiet time. You are also opening yourself to the assistance and healing energy available to you from all your guides and angels. If you can visualize the Spirit communication and healing energy that comes down to you through the top of your head and into your body, it will make sense how necessary it is to loosen tight neck and shoulder muscles that restrict the flow. By doing the Twenty-Second Meditation, you consciously relax those muscles, and all the extra help from your guides can freely flow through you.

You may not always be able to put your head in your hands, yet everyone has to breathe! So you can try one of the Breathing Meditations, in the next chapter, anyplace you need relaxation without anyone knowing what you are doing!

CHAPTER 4

The Breathing Meditations

Breathing in and breathing out being present in this moment. I separate from my physical self and become the witness. In this moment I find freedom within and bring it back into my life.

— *DAVID BENNETT, Voyage of Purpose*

The Breathing Meditation – Sensing the Air

1. Take three deep breaths, and with each exhalation feel your shoulders relax.
2. Return to your regular breathing.
3. Start to breathe in and out of your nose. If that is uncomfortable, you can also breathe in and out your mouth.
4. Place your attention on the sensation of the breath entering your nose or mouth. Feel the temperature and sense the air moving as it flows in.
5. When your mind wanders, don't judge it; simply start paying attention to your breath again.
6. Exhaling, place your awareness on the breath leaving your body.
7. Ignore how slow or fast you are breathing, what your posture is, or if anyone is looking! Everyone has to breathe. You don't look any different from the outside, except a little more relaxed.

8. Breathing in and out, pay attention to the sensation of your chest rising and falling as the air comes into and leaves your body.
9. Repeat for a minute or so and you'll feel the calming effect right away.
10. Add placing attention on your heartbeat, once you get good at focusing on your breath and your chest rising.

The Breathing Meditation – Counting

1. Take three deep breaths, relaxing your shoulders with each exhalation.
2. Return to your regular breathing.
3. Count slowly as you breathe in and then count slowly as you exhale. There is no "official" number of counts.
4. When your mind wanders, don't judge it; be gentle with yourself and start counting again.
5. Repeat for a minute or so and you'll start relaxing right away!

The Breathing Meditation – Counting When Sitting Down

1. Take three deep breaths, relaxing your shoulders with each exhalation.
2. Breathe in for the count of four; hold your breath for two and exhale for four; hold breath for two or pick a count that feels comfortable for you.
3. Continue to repeat the breath pattern: breath in, hold, breath out, and hold.
4. Gently go back to counting your breath if your mind wanders, don't judge it.
5. Repeat for a minute or so and you'll quickly feel centered.

WHERE AND WHEN

Breathing Meditations can be done anywhere, at almost any time. The best time for these meditations is when you want to calm your mind or get control of your body's knee-jerk reactions to stress. Are you stressing while waiting in line? Go ahead and do a Breathing Meditation. You can do it with your eyes open or closed. Can't sleep because your mind won't shut off? These meditations are great for releasing stress at any point of the day. I use Breathing Meditations when stuck at the doctor's office. I also do one when the nurse takes my blood pressure — and it is always healthy! Are your eyes getting stressed from too many hours on the computer? Just soften your gaze and do one of the Breathing Meditations. Dealing with traffic making you grumpy? You can do the Sensing the Air Breathing Meditation at the next stoplight. I also use the Breathing Meditation when I have to walk a long distance or am walking through the mall. I find it keeps me energized and makes the walk go by more quickly. I also do not get as winded. Do not do the Counting Breath and Sitting Down Meditations while standing up. You don't need to slow down your breath or hold it too long, and make sure you do not get up too quickly. Your body might not be used to getting that much oxygen and it can make you fuzzy headed.

EXAMPLE

Sean is on his way to watch his daughter at her baseball game and the traffic is painfully backed up. Sitting at the same light for the second time, without moving and with frustration building, he remembers the Sensing the Air Breathing Meditation. Sean figures he isn't going to get there any faster by getting angry. Instead he chooses to sense the breath coming in his nose and out his mouth. Even with the first few breaths he feels his shoulders relax and his mind stop racing. By the time the light turns green, it's his turn to go, and although he gets to the game at the third inning instead of the first, Sean is able to greet his daughter with a big smile, a shrug, and enjoy the rest of the game. Life happens.

WHY – THE IMPORTANCE OF BREATH

The average person takes about 19,000 breaths a day. That equals 50,000 gallons of air, which by weight is thirty-five times what you eat and drink. Powered by your heart, the oxygen is quickly distributed to your cells by your circulatory system. Without oxygen, your cells quickly die. Without breath, we cannot think or speak, let alone live.

Some researchers believe that slower breathing helps your circulation and even assists in breaking down the salt that you eat.[4] The well-known natural health doctor Andrew Weil has said that if he were limited to giving one healthy living tip, it would be to learn to breathe properly. Shallow breathing, which is how most people breathe when not aware of their breath, makes your body think it needs to activate the adrenal glands, producing stress hormones.[5] You can see why breathing deeply can be so important.

Most people do not breathe deeply. Normal lungs hold about two pints of air, yet most people take in a pint or less per breath. If you don't believe it, take a normal breath, see how much more air you can add to it, and then watch how you can add even more by lifting your shoulders. Fear, stress, and air pollution cause you to breathe shallowly. Poor posture, hectic lifestyle, and lack of concern for the ecosystem have compounded the problem. Yet remember that breathing is both voluntary and involuntary; you have the ability to increase the depth of your breath as well as steady its rhythm.

Rhythmic breathing will help you become more relaxed by taking you from the alert beta brain-wave state to the alpha state, which is considered a deeper level of relaxed consciousness. Alpha state is thought to naturally boost serotonin levels, relax the body and mind,[6] help with creativity, and assist your brain to process information better. Most people want all of that, especially the relaxation factor. Focusing on breathing deeply is the key.

Awareness of your breathing allows you to relax while taking stock of what your physical body is doing. Simply by taking deep, full breaths, your shoulders relax, and you become aware of your thoughts and energy.

Because everyone has to breathe, the Breathing Meditations are the most natural and easiest to accomplish in the middle of a crowd or when working at your desk. You won't look like you are doing anything different, yet little will those around you know, you are increasing your well-being and decreasing your stress!

SOUL SOOTHER

Entire systems of yoga have been built on focused breathing. Pranayama is one such practice, built on the belief that breath is one of the ways Divine Consciousness enters the body. Breath is also the primary tool to open the Heart Chakra. Your Heart Chakra is what allows you to take in and give love freely.

When you become aware of your breath, you are more in tune with your physical body. You know you are acting out of fear or stress when you are breathing shallowly. You can start to use your breath consciously to bring yourself back to the relaxed, focused, and balanced state that is the most productive for achieving your soul's goals. The alpha state is also helpful in accessing your intuition. Your soul often speaks through your intuition, and thus deep, rhythmic breathing is often the first major step to developing a better relationship with your soul. Your soul needs a healthy, energized body to work with. Deep, focused breathing has so many positive physical and emotional effects that you will be stronger and more prepared to keep up with your soul's life plan. In the next chapter you will learn the Grounding Meditations, which help you bring your intuition down to earth while connecting you to the energy needed to get through your busy day.

CHAPTER 5

The Grounding
Meditations

*When we rush forward without taking a moment to be centered
and present, our outcomes are less than whole. We are like a
cloud of probability, until we focus on this moment with
intention, then things move into alignment. With continued
focus we can achieve the outcomes that are our purpose.*

— *DAVID BENNETT*, *Voyage of Purpose*

The Grounding Meditation – Roots

1. Take three deep breaths, relaxing your shoulders with
   each exhalation.
2. Return to breathing normally.
3. Direct your awareness to your feet.
4. Imagine that strong and healthy roots are growing out
   of the soles of your feet and into the floor.
5. Envision them as super roots that can move through
   anything.
6. See them going deep into the earth. Feel the coolness of
   the earth.
7. Exhale as you send your frustration and any negativity
   you may have down through your roots, allowing the
   earth to absorb your tension.
8. Ask Mother Earth to cleanse and clear your roots and
   the ground below you.

9. Visualize your roots growing deeper and deeper into the earth until they reach a pool of nourishing Mother Earth energy at earth's center.
10. As you would draw up your favorite drink through a straw, imagine loving, nurturing Mother Earth energy rising up through your roots and into your legs.
11. Imagine Mother Earth energy constantly rising through your roots with each in-breath.
12. Be forgiving, yet firm each time your mind wanders.
13. Allow soothing energy to rise up first into your legs, relaxing each muscle it caresses as the energy continues to rise.
14. Breathe in, letting the energy continue up through your thighs, soothing and relaxing your muscles.
15. Let the soothing energy rise through your hips, relaxing all the muscles in your back and chest, as it bathes every cell in your body.
16. As Mother Earth energy reaches the top of your head, imagine it flowing up and out, like a fountain, and then pouring down the outside of your body. The circuit is completed as the nurturing energy flows back into the earth.
17. Thank Mother Earth and ask that all tension, frustration, or whatever you released be cleansed and returned to the earth as healing energy.
18. Allow yourself to retract your roots, yet leave a little of yourself in the earth so you stay grounded all day.

The Grounding Meditation – Red Cord
1. Take three deep breaths, relaxing your shoulders with each exhalation.
2. Return to breathing normally.

3. Instead of seeing roots growing out your feet, imagine a red cord coming from your tailbone.
4. Visualize your cord going deep into the earth. Just as a child gets its nourishment though its mother's umbilical cord, Mother Earth sends her nourishing energy to you all day through your red cord.
5. Imagine your cord going deeper into the earth and connecting itself to the center. You are not tethered like a leash. This cord freely moves, as you move.
6. Allow a moment to feel your connection with Mother Earth, sensing the energy that is being given to you. Know that you are being supported through this cord in the most nurturing way.
7. Think of your cord any time you feel low on energy and feel the energy flowing up from the earth and into the bottom of your spine.

WHERE AND WHEN

Either of these Grounding Meditations is great for when you feel tired, clumsy, or simply not focused. Often when your thoughts are ahead of where you are, like thinking of the long line at the post office when still walking out your door, you are not fully in your body. It is like you send a part of yourself into the future. Being ahead of yourself is a sure way to trip, bump into things, or forget where you parked. The Grounding Meditations help you stay in your body and in the present moment. First thing in the morning is an excellent time to ground. Other times for a Grounding Meditation are when you have an emotional situation to deal with — or even after you are done meditating! Some people like to ground after they finish work. Grounding in the parking lot or subway station is a simple way to let go of all the work stuff, get in the present moment, and move forward with the rest of your day. After the kids go to bed is another good grounding time. Grounding can be done sitting or standing yet it is best to avoid grounding when moving in a car or train until you have become comfortable with this meditation. If you have to fly, the Grounding Cord will work better than the Grounding Roots. Once you get good at it, try grounding while walking. Think of the Ent trees walking through the forest in *The Two Towers*, the second *Lord of the Rings* movie! You can stay grounded as you move throughout the day, keeping all of your energy in the present moment.

EXAMPLE

Gray is slightly late meeting her friend Nancy for a walk in the park, but she is a little tired and doesn't want to go without her cup of coffee. She drives right through one of the café's parking lot stop signs, but thank goodness, no one is there. She runs into the café, trips over the door jamb, and bumps into a café table. Ouch. Waiting in line, she realizes that she has been clumsy all day and decides to do a quick Grounding Meditation. The line isn't moving, but Gray decides the Grounding Cord Meditation is best because she hasn't yet gotten walking and rooting at the same time down. It only takes a minute to drop her red cord; she feels her body shift, become more balanced, energized, reconnected — and she is now next in line! Feeling grounded and refreshed, Gray decides she doesn't need the caffeine after all and chooses a healthier juice drink instead.

WHY - THE BENEFITS OF GROUNDING

Grounding is the process of connecting to earth's energy and bringing that energy into your body. Your ground can be thought of as your roots. Through the grounding process, you gain energy, nourishment, balance, power, security, stability, and spiritual growth.

Without grounding, you can become unstable and more susceptible to everyone else's energy rather than your own. When you lose your ground, you lose your ability to hold on to your own energy, which can leave you feeling powerless, confused, tired, and clumsy. When grounded, you feel supported, vitalized, and ready to accomplish everything on your to-do list. Sounds great, doesn't it? And it only takes minutes a day to accomplish! With the increase in your vitality, you can process common day-to-day stress with greater ease.

You become ungrounded when your thoughts are constantly in the future or the past. Understanding that energy goes where attention flows, you can see how your energy can end up in all sorts of places. Grounding is a technique that can help bring all your energy back to the present and your physical body. Any meditation in which you focus on the body can do this, yet grounding "roots" you in the present moment. Lack of protein and hydration can also leave you ungrounded, as well as too much time spent with people whose energy is not a good match for yours. Lack of sleep, or interrupted sleep, can unground you. You can see why grounding first thing in the morning can really start your day off right.

A simple solution for staying grounded besides using the Grounding Meditation is to get enough sleep. You have greater productivity during your day when you are well rested. When you wake up, take the time to stretch. Make a conscious effort to feel your feet, legs, hips, shoulders, arms, hands, and head. Also ensure you have enough protein and water throughout the day, wear more red colors, and spend time out in nature. You can keep crystals like garnet, black tourmaline, hematite, or bloodstone in your pocket. Why protein, water, red, crystals, and nature? It has to do with Chakras and the Energetic System that brings in and processes energy for your body. Protein is the food of the Root Chakra, which is where your connection to Earth is made.

UNIVERSAL ENERGY

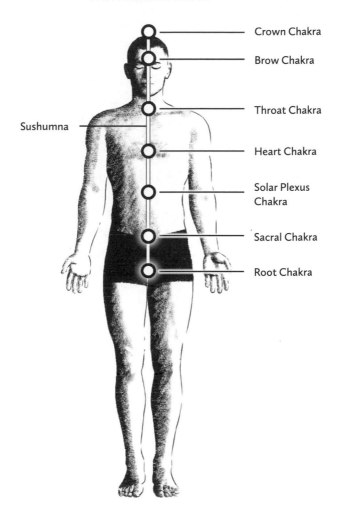

Crown Chakra

Brow Chakra

Throat Chakra

Sushumna

Heart Chakra

Solar Plexus
Chakra

Sacral Chakra

Root Chakra

EARTH ENERGY

Water is the food of the Sacral Chakra that is next in line, so if you do not get enough water, the energy won't flow smoothly to and from the Root Chakra. Red is the color of the Root Chakra and Earth is the element, so by wearing red and sitting in Nature, you are assisting the Root Chakra to absorb Earth's energy. The Crystals mentioned are only a few of the crystals that support the Root Chakra. A simple Web search will bring up more, or go to www.TwoHawksGallery.com where Dave or Lee can suggest crystals that support the Root Chakra or any of your chakras.

What is so important about Chakras and Earth's energy? Energy is what your body, mind, and spiritual connection works on. Your energy can be muddy or clear. The clearer your energy is, the better you feel and the stronger your intuition. Energy is very similar to food. As a matter of fact, a calorie is actually a measurement of energy. Think of muddy energy as empty calories, you won't get much from it. Your Chakras clean energy while moving it into, around, and out of the body. Although all energy is really the same, Earth and Spirit's energy are often thought of as a purer form of energy than another person's energy. There are seven main Chakras and their names and attributes differ depending on the culture. A simplistic yet effective way to think about them is as follows: the Root Chakra works mostly with Earth energy; the Sacral, Solar Plexus, Heart, Throat, and Brow Chakras deal more, though not exclusively, with the energetic exchanges between people and objects. The Crown Chakra is mostly involved with Spirit, or Universal Energy. If the chakras are working well, energy flows up and down the body, through a channel called the Sushumna. You can think of it as a highway running from the base of the spinal column to the top of the head with exits (the Chakras) that lead off to the organs and other parts of the body. If one of the Chakras is clogged up, it is like an exit closes on the highway; energy has to be rerouted and congestion forms. This type of energy congestion can create disease, so you can see why it is important to have the Chakras working well. More about Chakras will be discussed later, yet grounding is the first step to having a clear Sushumna (or highway). Being grounded is key to a well-balanced life, healthy Energetic System, and strong intuitive connection.

Grounding helps with hearing your intuition and sorting through your monkey mind-chatter. When you are grounded, you feel secure, energized, focused, and clear-minded. You are not influenced by outside energies or inner insecurities, allowing you to become more familiar with what your mind sounds like. Knowing your mind's "voice" assists you in easily distinguishing between what your mind and your intuition are telling you. You are also less likely to become delusional. You won't allow your mind to pretend it is your intuition. You will be centered, clear thinking, and able to recognize the difference between the two.

Grounding also protects your body from life's overloads. Energy can flow both in and out, so through grounding you can send the impact of your stress into the earth, a larger body that can handle it. It is like when a little boy needs to hold Mommy while the fireworks go off. He is grounding his stress into the mother. Mom, being a larger body, can absorb it without harm. Whether it is a loud noise, difficult person, or psychic vibration, there is a great deal of stress in your environment. Even happy events cause stress. Grounding is a way to cope with it all.

SOUL SOOTHER

When you are grounded and in the present moment, you become a clearer "channel" for your soul and intuition. You are less likely to misunderstand or twist what your intuition is telling you and more likely to be able to turn the guidance into practical advice. Your soul, guides, and angels want to communicate, and clearer communication is available to you when you are grounded. It is also important to be physically and energetically in the present moment. When your energy is in the present moment, your entirety is available for making the best choices and taking the best action when life suddenly throws you a curve ball. Choices you make today will affect how your tomorrow turns out. It is important that you live and make choices in ways that reflect your current situation rather than past issues.

Being grounded in the present moment allows you to make choices based on who you are today and with the full insight of your soul, guides, and angels. Yet even the most grounded person can't avoid unhealthy people and situations; the Staying in Your Energy Meditation, below, will help you to re-ground yourself when confronted with difficult people.

CHAPTER 6

The Staying-in-Your-Energy Meditation

*When we are mindful we can watch the trajectory of
our energy and watch the pattern it takes when we
interact with another, observe as our pattern goes up
or down or spiraling around.
At times we find our pattern matches someone or
a group and the resonance amplifies exponentially.
When we become an observer we become a soul in
wonder.*

— *DAVID BENNETT, Voyage of Purpose*

The Staying-in-Your-Energy Meditation

1. Stop and take a few deep breaths the next time you find yourself interacting with an unhealthy person or situation.

2. Close your eyes or look away from the person or situation for just a second if you cannot leave the area. You don't have to close your eyes or look away first, yet it will help you to detach.

3. Imagine that you are looking out from inside your head. If you have glasses on, notice the rims of the glasses. If you do not have glasses then imagine what it would look like to be behind your eyelashes.

4. Consciously make the decision to detach from the energy around you and continue to breathe deep and full.

5. Soften your gaze a little; you might want to practice softening your gaze in front of a mirror so you don't look dazed.

6. Pay attention to, and interact with, what is going on around you, but focus your energy tightly around your own body by staying behind your eyeglasses.

7. Breathe deeply if you feel energetically dragged into the situation again.

8. Find the best way to get yourself out of the unhealthy situation, while keeping your energy close to you by staying behind your eyelashes.

WHERE AND WHEN

The Staying in Your Energy Meditation proves you can practice meditation and still interact with your environment. It can be used when you are in any situation in which you feel that the energy around you is unhealthy. You don't always have to run away from these situations, yet it is important to evaluate the safest and most productive way to handle any given situation and person. This is easier when you are able to separate yourself from the situation's energy long enough to re-center. Often people choose this technique if they are dealing with someone who is angry or unbalanced. You will be able to think more clearly and be less affected by the energy around you. A crowded subway ride or office meeting where you can't get away from someone who is acting out is a perfect time to use the Staying in Your Energy Meditation. If you are in a heated discussion with someone, get behind your eyelashes and you won't find yourself as reactive and affected by his or her discordant energy. You don't have to look any different from before; this is an internal shift. You might feel like you are in your head and detached. This is okay for now. Stay there until you can remove yourself from the situation. I recommend this meditation to people who are going through a divorce, yet still living together, when each discussion can be more hostile than the last. It is also helpful when dealing with an overbearing parent, boss, or needy friend. Anytime you are feeling overwhelmed by another person's energy or an emotional situation, you can use the Staying in Your Energy Meditation.

It is important to be realistic about applying this meditation. You can only stay in this detached space for a short while. This meditation is to be used as a way to help you detach from unhealthy energy long enough to reconnect to your own energy, your soul's goals, and see your best next move. Sometimes that can mean a permanent move away from the unhealthy job, relationship, or neighborhood.

EXAMPLE

Sandy is dreading dinner with her mother today. She feels guilty about it; her mom is so negative, always dumping all of her drama on Sandy. Sandy is usually exhausted after these dinners and her stomach often gives her trouble as a result. Today she picks up her mother at her assisted-living residence a few minutes early to avoid having to listen to her mom complain that she is late. As soon as Sandy's mom gets into the car, the complaining starts. This time it is about the neighbor leaving his garbage in the hallway. Sandy feels trapped in the car and doesn't know if she can deal with a whole dinner of this. Once her mother finds something to complain about, she doesn't let go (though at least it isn't about Sandy being late!). Sandy's stomach begins to flip-flop as they walk into the restaurant. They sit across from each other and her mother starts going on about how the food at the home is terrible. Sandy decides to try the positive approach, cheerfully pointing out that her mother is sure to get a good meal tonight! It goes right over her mother's head as she continues to complain about last night's overcooked broccoli.

Sandy decides to try the Staying in Your Energy Meditation and begins by looking at her mother from behind her glasses. Immediately, she realizes how much her energy has become entwined with her mother's negative energy. Just by detaching a little from the conversation, Sandy can breathe easier. She realizes that her breath had become shallow, a knee-jerk protection from breathing in too much of her mother's cynicism. Sandy looks at her mom from behind her glasses and allows her gaze to soften. Her mother doesn't look quite as old and Sandy is reminded of when the two of them used to sneak away shopping while her other siblings and father went to baseball games. Sandy and her mother had never liked baseball and so they relished that special time together. That was before her mother turned so sour, yet Sandy can see how her mother's complaining about the food at the home is similar to how she talked about not liking baseball. Back then, however, Sandy's mother took control of her life to do things she enjoyed. Her complaints were not so negative then; they were more like having an opinion, making choices. Sandy's whole body relaxes as she realizes that she too has a choice on how to deal with her mother's negativity and that she also can do something different. Sandy takes control of the situation and her energy. She takes a deep breath, grounds, and asks her mother what they can do about the food at the home. The two of them come up with ideas for a letter they will write to the management. Both Sandy and her mother feel better. Sandy's mom even comments that the center's cooks should take some cooking lessons from this restaurant and proceeds to rave about her dinner the whole ride home.

WHY – ENERGETIC EXCHANGE BETWEEN PEOPLE

Plain and simple, other people's energy affects us. Think of someone's energy spreading out like the smell of cookies baking in the oven. When you walk into a house where someone is baking cookies, you smell them the minute you enter the door. You might even start to feel hungry. A person, or even a place's energy, can be sensed before you can see the source of it, and it can affect you from a distance as well. Right now, think of the last time you had fresh-baked, warm, delicious-smelling cookies right out of the oven. Even though you do not really smell them now, you might even find your mouth watering or your tummy reacting. Energy works like that, too! Your energy goes where your attention is focused, and you experience the energy that is manifested where you are focused. That energy affects you and how you react in a current situation. Energy can affect you from the past, present, or even projected into the future. For example, if you are thinking of when you broke up, and at the time you felt that the energy was very discordant, then you bring that discordant energy into your present moment. You and those you are dealing with in the present moment will be affected by the past discordant energy.

This is why it can be so destructive to keep reliving a distressing experience. You keep re-bathing yourself in the unhealthy energy of that experience. Our ability to experience energy by thinking of past situations enables us to reminisce. That can be a boost when it is a positive memory, yet obsessing about a past unhealthy situation can be very detrimental.

When you are in close quarters with someone with destructive energy, the effect is compounded because when you interact with someone, your energies become deeply entwined. The process of going behind your eyelashes helps to detach you from his or her energy. It does not remove you one hundred percent, yet it can assist you in reclaiming your center and help create a healthier boundary between the two of you.

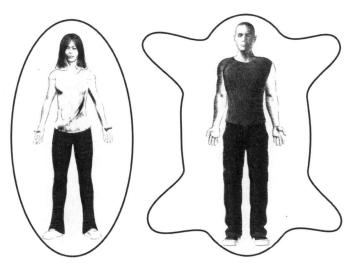

Energy Condensed   Energy Invasive

You do not want to live detached from other people's energies — life would get boring pretty quickly. The Staying in Your Energy Meditation is to be used when you cannot get out of a difficult situation. This meditation also helps you to realize how you are affected by other people's energies and, in turn, how you affect others. To be mindful of how your energy affects others is an important part of spiritual growth. Another reason to not stay detached is that sharing energies can feed each other in a positive way. Think of how wonderful you feel after getting together for a cup of tea with a positive friend. The two of you both walk away feeling terrific! It is more than the good company; there has been an energetic exchange. Yet that exchange can backfire just as easily, resulting in feeling drained after an exchange with a needy or difficult person.

It is not always the other person's energy that affects you. You can send part of your own energy away by focusing on a person or situation. Remember that energy flows where attention goes, so thinking about a situation or person is like feeding it. In a healthy relationship, both partners send energy back and forth.

PEOPLE SHARING ENERGY

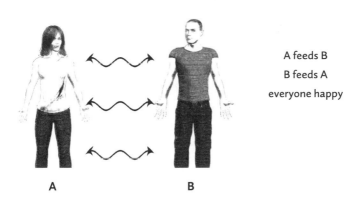

A feeds B
B feeds A
everyone happy

A   **B**

Take the example of a woman dealing with a relationship breakup. When she has trouble letting go of the other person, she obsesses about him. It is like sending an energetic sandwich, every time you think about him. She feels drained, but her ex-boyfriend feels great. He doesn't know why, he just does. He may even think it is the freedom of not being in a relationship that has him so charged; yet it is the woman delivering her energy to him like a pizza.

PEOPLE SHARING ENERGY

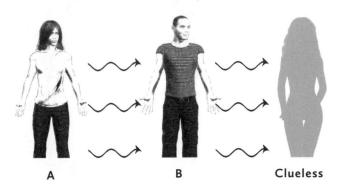

A obsessing and feeding B – B interested and feeding C
A hungry and tired – B doesn't notice difference

Eventually she starts to get over the relationship. She is not thinking of her ex so much, and even starts to flirt with someone new! She is no longer sending her energy to the ex.

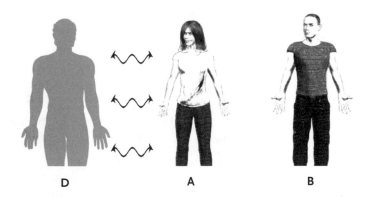

A now thinking of D – B gets hungry because A looks
back to D for energy

Now, doesn't it figure, her ex calls her up, just as she is starting to move on. She thinks, "Wow, he must have missed me so much —

he will be a much better boyfriend now!" Sorry, but most of the time, it is the energetic sandwich he is missing. The old relationship issues are still there.

I am not saying that every time a relationship resumes it is doomed because of this energetic exchange. Yet I have seen it happen over and over again in my spiritual counseling practice. The best way to make sure you don't fall into the same dead-end cycle after a relationship ends is to go out and do things that you enjoy, reminding yourself of your potential. Make yourself the focus of your energy instead of feeding it to the ex. Sometimes it is helpful to have a "go-to" image or daydream to use when you find yourself obsessing about the old relationship. Maybe pick someplace you would love to visit, and when you think of the ex, shift your thoughts to your new image. Another technique is to see yourself surrounded in Golden Light, God's unconditional love, coming from above. Ask your guides or angels to arrange that your ex's guides surround him in his own Golden Light. You don't want the energy to come from you, or to merge your Golden Lights, as that would defeat the purpose. An image for this is on the next page.

Another way to avoid being drained by difficult people and situations is to understand them as story lines in your life's play. If you believe that before you incarnate your soul works out a life story that will teach you what you need to learn and offer you the experiences you wish to have, it is easy to imagine that these difficult people and situations are a part of your story line. Taking as an example an everyday scenario, imagine that the obnoxious lady at the Customer Service desk is there because you asked her to teach you patience. Instead of looking at her as someone whose life purpose is to torment you today, imagine that your soul prearranged this scene in order for you to practice being as patient as possible. Often when you learn your desired lesson, the difficult situation

Angel giving
each person energy
separately

(or person) leaves. This is not to say you should stay in a dysfunctional relationship, job, or home life because it is teaching you lessons. That is not the way it works. These types of situations arise in your life's play to cue you that it's time for movement and growth. When you understand the lesson, you make the changes in your life to reflect the learning. Don't worry, if you didn't get it right or missed part of it, your guides will make sure to present the lesson again in a way that allows you to be more successful! Choosing suffering is not expected, required, useful, or necessary for growth.

Recognizing that not every person's action or reaction has to do with you is another way not to get knocked about by situations with people. Our human tendency is to think everything is always about us. When you start to realize that the obnoxious Customer Service person is most likely obnoxious to everyone, or that the guy who boxed your car in is simply a poor driver, you don't need to waste your energy on the situation. This does not release you of the responsibility of how your own energy may contribute to a situation, yet most often other people's reactions have little to do with you. The Attitude Adjuster Meditation will go deeper in how to work with your own energy. Yet, simply said, your energy affects others as much as their energy affects you, so being aware of your energy can assist you in having a positive influence on any unhealthy situation.

SOUL SOOTHER

Your soul wants you to grow. The knowledge you gain through your interactions with others is one of the reasons you incarnated. Yet often self-sacrifice, fear, and the overwhelming affect of others creates a situation of stagnation. Learning doesn't happen when you stay in a weak position; the lessons come when you rise out of the muck and stand on your own two feet. This is not to say you always need to be in control of every situation; that is not possible. Instead, there is a great lesson to be learned from being able to give in. Giving in is for those who have trouble letting go of control, not for those unable to establish it. Similarly, standing up for yourself is an important lesson for those who have trouble with that, not for the person who leans toward the overbearing side. Become balanced by knowing your weak and strong points. Work toward strengthening what attributes you are missing and not letting your weak points make your decisions for you. What you need to become a well-rounded and whole person will be presented to you in one form or another — repeatedly, in fact, until you learn the lesson!

Your soul wants you to be able to find yourself and re-center in the midst of a difficult situation. Gaining the ability to detach from someone else's energy is often key to being able to do just that. Sometimes you simply need to walk away from an unhealthy situation, and you'll find a meditation for when you walk in the next chapter.

CHAPTER 7

The Walking Meditations

Listen deeply to the rhythm of your heartbeat and breath,
notice how the whole body relaxes with deep listening.
It causes cooperation between our conscious mind and
our higher self. The more we practice deep listening the
farther inward we go toward stillness.

— *DAVID BENNETT, Voyage of Purpose*

The Walking Meditation – Sensation

1. Take three deep breaths, and with each exhalation, sense your shoulders relaxing.
2. Return to breathing normally.
3. Decide where you are walking. Sounds silly, but doing so avoids having to think about where you are going while doing your walking meditation.
4. Realize that you are walking and that this is your only important task right now.
5. Start walking, and pay attention to the sensation of your feet touching the ground. You don't have to look at them, just feel the sensation.
6. Return to sensing your feet making contact with the ground if your mind wanders.
7. Become aware of whether you are a heel-toe walker or a toe-heel walker.

8. Allow all your attention to be focused on your walking. (Except put a little aside to make sure you don't walk into someone or cross a street without looking!)

9. Try to stay mindful for the whole walk. If you do, you'll arrive peaceful, relaxed, and focused.

The Walking Meditation – Adding the Breath

1. Take three deep breaths, and with each exhalation, allow your shoulders to relax.

2. Return to breathing normally.

3. Decide where you are walking.

4. Remember that *walking* is your only important task at this moment.

5. Sense your feet making contact with the ground, as you did in the Sensation Walking Meditation.

6. Go back to sensing your feet if you start to think of your list of things to do.

7. Become aware of your breath without loosing focus on your feet.

8. As you inhale through the nose, bring Earth energy in, up through your feet. As you exhale, release any tension you might have up and out of your mouth.

9. Continue your awareness of your breath and feet.

10. Notice your walking rhythm. It isn't necessary to slow down unless you realize your rhythm is uncomfortable.

11. Allow all your attention — except leave some to make sure you don't walk into someone or cross a street without looking — to be focused on your walking and breathing.

12. Keep your attention on your walking and breath until you arrive at your location or reach your desired level of mindfulness.

The Walking Meditation – Enjoying Nature

1. Find a pleasant green space or place in Nature. It does not matter if it is crowded or noisy.
2. Take three deep breaths, and with each exhalation, experience your shoulders relaxing more and more.
3. Return to breathing normally.
4. Realize that you are walking, and that this is your only important task right now.
5. Become aware of walking with Nature, not through it. You and Nature share this space.
6. Make the conscious effort to connect to the Earth. Silently say "Earth" each time you step down.
7. When your mind wanders, don't judge yourself. Return your attention to your walking and labeling "Earth" as each foot touches the ground.
8. Notice if you start to walk more softly.
9. Expand your attention to the sounds around you as you keep your attention on your feet connecting with the Earth. No need to judge the sounds as good or bad; label them simply as "child," "bird," "yelling" — or what ever sound you encounter.
10. Continue your mindful walking.
11. Include the rhythm of your breathing if you feel ready.
12. Allow all your attention to be dedicated to your walking, listening, and breathing, yet be aware of safety.
13. If your mind wanders, simply, without self-judgment, return your attention back to your walking, breathing, and listening.
14. Take a minute to ground and bring your attention back to your body when you are done walking.

WHERE AND WHEN

We don't all have the opportunity to stroll in nature, so where else can you do the Walking Meditation? Try it when walking from your car to the store. Don't think about what you are shopping for; just apply your attention to your walking. You can do this at work, too, on the way to a meeting or to the restroom. We all have to walk somewhere! Of course, a forest is a soothing place to do any Walking Meditation, but if you live in a concrete jungle, you can find green spaces, or be near a river or fountain, to do your walking. A mall or office building will often have green space and in the early morning you'll probably find other walkers. You can even practice the Walking Meditation at home. Try it on the way to bed and notice how your mind-chatter will less likely keep you awake. If you were to do the Walking Meditations during just one-quarter of your walking time, you would get stress release and add calm to a large part of your day. Don't worry if at first you walk funny. You have not paid attention to your feet in a long time.

TIP: You can use this technique anywhere, not just walking. Are you at your desk all day on the computer? As you type, pay attention to your fingers on the keys along with the words you type or the clicking of the keys.

EXAMPLE

Pax is driving around the mall, looking for a close parking spot. She feels grumpy and annoyed about having to go back to the store to have the security tag removed from the pants she bought last night. Pax is sure the Parking Lot Angels aren't listening today, because the closest parking spot she finds is far from the entrance. As she sets out on foot to the doors, something reminds her of the Walking Meditation. She starts sensing her steps: "Heel, Toe."

"Heel, Toe." Suddenly she lets out a long sigh and realizes how tense she is about having to go back to the mall today: "Heel, Toe." "Heel, Toe." She notices the cool breeze on her face and the sun shining: "Heel, Toe." "Heel, Toe." She realizes she hasn't been getting any exercise lately with her busy schedule and decides to park a little farther out from now on. The Parking Lot Angels watch Pax with big smiles, knowing their message got through this time.

WHY – MINDFULNESS

Walking Meditation teaches you to focus in the present moment, training you to be mindful. Nearly every time I teach a class on spirituality, the lesson seems to come down to being mindful. Virtually every mistake I make could have been avoided or minimized if mindfulness had come into play. What is mindfulness? My favorite definition is: the state of being in tune with oneself and one's environment.

Does that mean all you have to do is focus more on what you're doing? Paying attention is part of focus and focus is a part of being mindful. Yet focus narrows your awareness, putting your attention on a single thing while mindfulness expands your awareness to include many things. Focus is the first step in the path to mindfulness; meditation is the second step.

Often books on the subject of mindfulness are really on the practice of meditation. Meditation is a great tool. Meditation has a tendency to take us *away* from the clutter of everyday life whereas mindfulness brings the meditative state directly *inside* the clutter of everyday life.

You may find that when practicing mindfulness, you have to slow down and do things more purposefully. Although you may feel you don't have time to slow down, in reality, by being mindful, you're saving time in the long run!

Consider my coffee experience in the morning. Almost every time I pour the first cup of coffee out of the coffeemaker, I spill it. When I am mindful, pouring it slowly and paying close attention, I don't spill, which means I don't have to take the time to get the rag to clean up my spilled coffee. I realize this might be a silly example, but it comes from real life. How much time do you spend looking for your keys? If you were being mindful when you placed the keys down, you would be able to remember where you left them. For a while, I consciously made the effort to be mindful about where I put my keys when I came into the house. You'd be surprised how well it worked! Being mindful leads to having more time and energy each day because you won't be wasting so much of it cleaning up coffee and looking for keys.

When you are mindful, each movement has purpose and is used to its full advantage. You can see what pulls your energy and what helps save your energy. No longer running around in circles, you are more effective at what you do, leaving more time to relax and recharge. You are going with the flow of your environment, not against it.

Intuitive connection is also easier when there isn't so much mind-chatter to distract you. Your mind can be like a party and your intuition like a whisper. As my mother's pastor said in one of his sermons, "How can you hear God answering your prayers if you don't stop talking long enough to listen?"

With mindfulness, you are connected to the natural flow of life, so when opportunities come that can move you toward a better tomorrow, you are listening enough to pick up on them. When your actions start to create a tomorrow that isn't in accord with the natural flow, you'll notice quickly enough to stop your actions — or at least have time to do damage control. Mindfulness is something that you develop slowly and do better as you keep working on it. You can't expect to be mindful in a flash, as you didn't become mindless in a flash. Don't judge yourself or others harshly: gaining mindfulness is a process.

By now you probably see the advantage of being mindful and are willing to risk trying it. Here are some ways to work on adding mindfulness into your life:

1. Try adding the Walking Meditations, or any of the meditations in this book, into your daily routine.
2. Be willing to see the good, the bad, and the ugly in yourself and others.
3. Start paying more attention to your mind, and acknowledge how out of control it can be.
4. Make a commitment to not judge yourself or others. Just take note of what you see and leave it at that.
5. Did I say stop judging yourself and others? It bears repeating since non-judgment is the most important tool in your mindfulness tool bag.

SOUL SOOTHER

As in the example, Pax is able to hear guidance from the Parking Lot Angels better when she practices her Walking Meditation. Mindfulness brings an expanded awareness that allows your soul, guides, and angels to communicate; yet it is so much more than that. As you become more mindful, you find that you are going with the flow of life instead of fighting against it. I love the analogy of the fish that keeps fighting the current to stay where it is. The fish spends all day fighting and fighting, and when finally exhausted, not able to fight the current any longer, the fish is swept up by the current to a pond at the end of the river that is calm, full of food, and other fish. Often we are that fish, not mindful of how the current is exhausting us, and unaware of what opportunities our soul, guides, and angels have created for us if we would simply let go. Mindfulness may not show us the pond, yet it will allow us to be aware that there is a flow leading us to another place that could be less stressful and full of opportunity.

Another meditation to help with mindfulness is the Bell Meditation.

CHAPTER 8

The Bell
Meditation

*Take a minute to breathe in this moment like a new
book.. Ahhh the freshness of a new beginning where we
can create positive change for our world and let it
dawn within. Let us author peace, understanding
and happiness. Reach out a hand of help to those in need,
by helping others we help ourselves. Let us shine our
lights and greet this new moment.*

— DAVID BENNETT, *Voyage of Purpose*

The Bell Meditation

1. Choose a sound or action that you hear or experience at least
   five times a day. An action could be using your debit card, and
   a sound might be your cell phone ringing.
2. Every time your sound or action occurs, take a deep breath.
   The phone will still be there if you wait one extra ring.
3. Pay attention to where your mind is. Are you thinking about
   what you are doing now, or is your mind in the past or future?
   Are your thoughts calm or agitated? Don't judge yourself,
   simply note your thoughts, take a deep breath, and shift them
   if they need it
4. Pay attention to your body. Is your breathing shallow or
   deep? Are your shoulders tensed or relaxed? Are you sitting
   or standing correctly? Are you slumped over?

5. Fix anything that might be adversely affecting your body.
6. Pay attention to your surroundings. Are you being affected by outside influences?
7. Note how you are being affected and if possible, fix it.
8. Go back to what you are doing. Bring your newfound mindfulness into your activity.

WHERE AND WHEN

Use this mini-meditation to practice mindfulness throughout your day. The Bell Meditation is a reminder to come back to the state of mindfulness. When you hear your "bell," check in to see where your mind is. Each time it "rings," take a deep breath and connect with your mind, body, and environment. Bring yourself back to the present moment and mindfulness. Don't judge what you find when you check in; simply note it. The Bell Meditation is great for work. You can make any sound or activity into a bell as long as it isn't happening constantly.

A receptionist might not want to make a phone ringing into a bell, yet for someone who only gets calls a few times a day, it is perfect. The receptionist could use the mail delivery along with a trip to the copier as bells. If you are a busy mom, you could use walking through the doorway to the kitchen as your bell, or every time you get in or out of the car. Eventually your bell will get stale and loose its effectiveness and so you may need to change it a bit. If you are a person who gets caught up in the moment, loses track of time, obsesses, or whose physical disabilities are aggravated when you don't pay attention to your body, this is a perfect meditation to keep you in touch with your thoughts, body, and environment. The Bell Meditation will assist any time you need to bring mindfulness into your daily life.

EXAMPLE

Dave is an author who travels, and between writing, websites, and social networking, spends a lot of time on his computer. He doesn't get phone calls often; most people contact him via email. So a ringing phone does not work well as a bell. He also has a rebuilt spine and working at the computer can be quite painful. He wants to develop a bell so that he is reminded to get up and stretch as well as be mindful about how he is sitting. Since he travels, he needs a bell he can carry with him. He found an app for his iPhone that actually has a bell that he can set to go off a number of times a day. Dave is working at home today. When the iPhone bell goes off, he takes a deep breath, and puts his attention to where his thoughts are. His thoughts are positive and in the present moment, so he moves his attention to his body. He discerns that he is sitting in his chair cockeyed and his neck hurts. He stands up to stretch his muscles. Realizing that his neck pain is from the angle he was holding his head, he takes a few minutes to raise the computer monitor a couple of inches. Dave returns to working on the website, noting how much better his neck feels with the monitor adjusted.

WHY – DISCERNMENT VS. JUDGMENT

As discussed in the chapter on the Walking Meditation, adding mindfulness to your life offers you the ability to get off autopilot and back in your mind's driver seat. Mindfulness helps you to be proactive instead of reactive, while compelling you to take responsibility for your actions. Yet, practicing mindfulness can also set you up to start judging yourself. You have enough people judging you without doing it yourself. This doesn't mean that everything you do is fine, and that you are perfect, it only means that judging is not a productive way to institute change.

The human tendency is to judge what is experienced as either good or bad. This person is not nice, so he or she must be bad. This ice cream tastes rich and creamy, so it must be good. Many spiritual teachings emphasize the importance of being able to separate what you experience from how you feel about it. You can then decide if it is in your best interest, without judging it as good or bad. For example, decadent ice cream with all the sugar and calories may make the taste buds happy, and you say, "This is really good." Yet if you eat too much of it, you may find the first rush of pleasure turning into a sugar crash. That sugar rush may feel good or bad depending on how your body processes sugar. Yet to deal with all that sugar, your pancreas pumps out a lot of insulin, challenging your immune system. Sleep will be difficult tonight and your immune system will take 24 hours to get back to normal, so you think the ice cream is bad. But when you look at this situation more closely, it isn't the ice cream that is good or bad. The ice cream is simply ice cream. It is how your body feels after eating it that makes you decide if it is good or bad. Spiritual teachings suggest that you don't label the ice cream at all. It is ice cream, not good or bad — it just is.

Looking at things as they are, without judging them, is called *discernment*. Your mind tends to judge; your intuition uses discernment. Your intuition looks at your situation, along with the most likely outcome of your options, to see which choice leads you closer to your soul's path. In the case of ice cream, your intuition would not say it is good or bad, yet it might *discern* that if you have a little of it, maybe a kiddie-sized cone, the sugar in the ice cream cone won't send you on quite the same sugar high and inevitable crash as the double cone you contemplate getting. That discerning choice will allow you to have the kiddie cone and still get to the tasks you need to later on, without falling asleep because of a sugar crash.

A wonderful story of discernment is about a monk looking out a window. He sees the sun shining, a slight breeze, and puffy white clouds. He exclaims, "This is going to be a great day: the flowers will benefit from the sun!" He grabs a light sweater and begins his walk to the garden for fresh vegetables. The next day he looks out the window and it is raining, a little cold, and a stiff breeze is coming from the north. He exclaims, "This is going to be a great day: the flowers will benefit from the rain!" The monk grabs his boots, coat, and umbrella for his walk to the garden. This monk's story teaches three things: 1) weather is neither good nor bad; 2) don't let the rain determine if you are going to have a great day; and 3) be prepared and don't forget your umbrella.

All of life offers lessons and opportunities for growth. Allowing yourself the freedom to live without judgment, yet with a strong ability to discern what is best for your highest and most loving good, allows you to make choices throughout your day to create the best environment for growth. Using the Bell Meditation gives you the opportunity to stop living in autopilot mode, and allows you to take control of how you choose to participate in your environment.

After a while of practicing discernment, you will stop making limiting choices based on short-term thinking and begin to make choices that bring you into balance and are best for your long-term goals. Discernment doesn't tell you that you can never have a double-scoop ice-cream cone. It simply helps you choose a time when the sugar crash won't get in your way of accomplishing your soul's goals — and it reminds you to bring the umbrella in case it rains!

SOUL SOOTHER

Your soul knows that judgment is a waste of time, yet with discernment you can change what is not working in your life to create an environment around you that promotes the most soul growth.

Judgment often creates an adverse vibrational state while discernment is neutral. Living a discerning life allows a more optimistic outlook. You are not living in fear of "bad" things happening as you realize that it is natural for life to present challenges. You stay open to whatever solutions are available rather than shutting down out of pessimism; you'll feel optimistic, yet realistic, about what needs to be done. Discernment creates an opportunity for you to think about what you want in your life, how you want to act, what type of energy and vibrations you want around you, see situations and people as they truly are, and make choices that lead you closer to fulfilling your potential.

Your soul wants you to be able to discern the energy and vibrations that are not for your highest and loving good. One way to do that is by using the Blessing Meditation to send loving energy to anyone or any situation you encounter that might need a little extra vibratory boost.

CHAPTER 9

The Blessing Meditations

If we start each day with gratitude and stillness then our walk through the day becomes one of connection to everything. We can bring the sacred into our everyday tasks. When we do, we see what is really important and focus on our core roles. Our every thought and action affects the fabric of creation and thus our future tomorrows. Let's treat each moment with sacred respect and vitalize the ceremony of life.

— *DAVID BENNETT, Voyage of Purpose*

The Blessing Meditation – For People

1. Take a deep breath and feel your shoulders relax as you exhale.
2. Return to breathing normally.
3. Think of someone you love and want only the best for. It is best to choose someone you're not in a romantic situation with, especially if complications are associated with the relationship. I might choose my sister.
4. Allow the love you feel for that person to strengthen and coalesce in your heart.
5. Spend a moment with this loving sensation.
6. Increase that love as you see it forming into a golden ball of light.

7. Silently bless people as you come across them using whatever phrase feels comfortable. Simply say, "Bless you," or if you know the person, silently say, "Bless you, [name]."

8. Send out your golden ball of loving light, from your heart, toward the person. Intend that your blessing be received in a way that is for the highest and most loving good.

9. Making eye contact is not necessary, yet if you feel like it, you can offer a friendly smile.

10. Imagine your blessing floating his or her way, knowing that if he or she needs the blessing or loving feeling, it will be received. There is no need to force your blessing on the person.

11. Ask the golden ball of light to be dispersed into the area, if the person is not open to receiving at this time.

12. Continue with your day, silently blessing people as you come across them.

The Blessing Meditation – For Situations in the Future

1. Take a deep breath and feel your shoulders relax as you exhale.

2. Return to breathing normally.

3. Think of a situation that had a loving outcome.

4. Feel the love created through that situation.

5. Allow the love you felt then to strengthen and coalesce in your heart.

6. Spend a moment with that loving sensation.

7. Increase that love as you see it forming into a golden ball of light.

8. Imagine the situation that you are going to be entering, in your mind's eye.

9. Bless this situation and send the loving golden ball of light into the future to create a loving energy around the upcoming situation.

10. Intend your blessing to be received in a way that is for the highest and most loving good.
11. Ask if any of the persons involved in the situation are not open to receiving at this time, the golden ball of light disperse into the future assisting the future situation to have a higher vibration.
12. Let go of worrying, as it will only drain you and send worry energy into the situation.

The Blessing Meditation – For Situations in the Present Moment
1. Take a deep breath and feel your shoulders relax as you exhale.
2. Return to breathing normally.
3. If you can't take a deep breath, at least focus on your breath for a moment.
4. Think of a situation where you know the outcome was for the highest and most loving good. It is best to choose a situation that creates a loving feeling into your heart, like when a loved one was healed or a child was born.
5. Allow the feeling of love you felt to strengthen and coalesce in your heart.
6. Take a second to feel that loving sensation.
7. Increase that love as you see it forming into a golden ball of light.
8. Ask that blessings be sent to the current situation using whatever phrase feels comfortable. I simply say, "Bless this situation."
9. Intend your blessing to be received in a way that is for the highest and most loving good.
10. Send out your golden ball of loving light from your heart, toward all who are involved in the current situation.

11. You do not need to make eye contact with the other persons involved in the current situation, or even be in the same room as those involved.
12. Imagine your blessing floating toward all those concerned.
13. Intend the golden ball of light to help the entire situation have a higher vibration, if any of the persons involved in the situation are not open to receiving at this time.

WHERE AND WHEN

Going to and from work is a great time to practice the Blessing Meditation. You can use the Blessing People Meditation as you come in contact with people or the Blessing a Future Situation Meditation when you are on your way home, sending loving energy to the home. When you find yourself in a difficult meeting at work or dealing with a difficult home situation, sending loving energy in a non-pushy way can set a more positive tone and allow others to access a level of compassion that they may not be able to on their own. There is no need to force your blessing on the situation. Know that if they are open to it, and it will benefit the situation, the loving energy will be received. You can even send the blessing to yourself — in the future or past.

There are no limitations about when and where to use these Blessing Meditations as long as you intend the energy to be used for the highest and most loving good and do not force the blessing. You can imaging laying the blessing on a silver platter, setting it in front of the person and allowing him or her to take it or not. Doing blessings this way respects the person's vibratory rate and personal space. Blessings are not limited to people. For instance, I have found that if there is an area of clutter that I cannot control, or am having trouble bringing myself to clean, instead of cursing it every time I walk by I bless it.

EXAMPLE

Anne is working on her Heart Chakra and bringing more compassion into her daily life. She decides that today she will bless everyone she comes in contact with. A tall order, yet Anne is gentle with herself and attempts to do her best. She has a lot of errands today and starts at the grocery store, walking up and down the aisles, silently blessing each person she passes. Each time she blesses someone else she feels the love within her grow. Feeling good she leaves the store, and heads to her next stop to straighten out a problem with her son's bank account. She knows that the woman at the bank is not easy to deal with so she sends a blessing to the bank lady in advance, as well as to the situation in general. Anne feels a calm come over her as she enters the bank, smiling, and she thanks herself for the extra loving energy!

The bank woman remains difficult, Anne realizes that her little golden ball of blessing light might not be enough to make this usually cranky woman any softer in one day, yet blesses her again. The bank lady doesn't give in, yet Anne is not getting as annoyed as usual. She resigns herself to the fact that the bank woman will not bend the rules, and that she must bring her son with her to make the changes to his account. Her next stop is to see her friend Sharon, who is working at Anne's favorite consignment shop. Sharon has been having a tough time lately, so Anne sends her a blessing before walking in the door. Sharon tells Anne how down in the dumps she was and how, just thinking of Anne a moment ago, she immediately felt better! They have a wonderful chat and Anne leaves feeling blessed herself, as if the blessing has bounced right back.

WHY – GRATITUDE IS THE ATTITUDE

The Blessing Meditation can benefit you as much as those who receive the blessing. You must fill yourself with loving energy before you can send it out, and that love will stay with you as well. You will find that there is almost never a time when the Blessing Meditations cannot be used.

The Blessing Meditation in a situation, either current or in the future, can help alleviate your anxiety as well as promote a calmer, more loving energy for everyone involved to pull from. The act of blessing brings you into a sacred place of appreciation and love. The best way to bring gratitude and love into your day is to share it with others.

Gratitude is an important lesson for anyone on the spiritual path. If one of my clients is suffering from depression, and is also involved in taking care of the physical side of their well-being, I suggest that he or she not get out of bed without thinking of one thing to be grateful for. Sometimes a person who is feeling down has trouble thinking of anything. I suggest using, "I am grateful that I woke up this morning," and then look out for things during the day that might work for tomorrow. When I use the Blessing Meditation I find that at first I might say something silly, like "I am grateful I got my favorite seat at the café." Often, after a few days, my gratitude gets deeper. I eventually find an abundance of things to be grateful for and have trouble picking just one.

Gratitude helps open you to the possibilities being offered to you, allowing you to be in a space of anticipation and awareness of all that is Life. You don't have to wait until life is perfect to practice gratitude. No one has a life without bumps in the road. My husband, David Bennett, had cancer and still did a meditation to express gratitude every day. People thought he was crazy to be grateful for the cancer. Yet he feels that because of his cancer and resulting back surgeries, he was given the ability and opportunity to write *Voyage of Purpose*. As a survivor of Stage IV lung cancer, David continues to be of service by offering hope and inspiration to others who might not be able to see their way through such a difficult diagnosis.

I want to make a bumper sticker, "Gratitude Is the Attitude!" I use gratitude every time I write a check. I am grateful that the money is there, even if I am just squeaking by. When I write out the dollar amount on the check, instead of putting zeros under the cents, I put XXXX and say aloud, "God is my supply." I even have that phrase printed on my checks! As I rip the check from the pack, I thank Spirit for the abundance and send the check along with the energy of abundance and gratitude instead of dread and resentment.

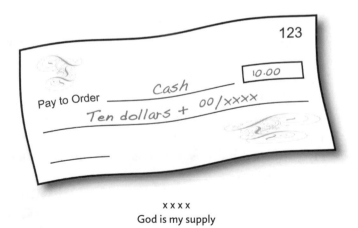

x x x x
God is my supply

I also try to express this gratitude each time I sign my debit card, thinking, "God is my supply" while signing my name. My mindfulness is not as good at the register — I simply do it each time I remember.

Recognizing that similar energies are attracted to each other, you may find that the more you practice gratitude, the more likely you are going to attract people with the same positive attitude. It is through the Blessing Meditations that you can develop a deep appreciation for all of life becoming the basis for your attitude of gratitude.

SOUL SOOTHER

The more that you use the Blessing Meditation, the more you activate your soul's light and shine it into your environment. By blessing someone, you are doing more than sharing a loving vibration, you are asking the Universe to bring that person or situation into harmony with all that is for the highest and most loving good.

Doing the Blessing Meditation offers people and situations an example of a higher vibration to emulate, giving the opportunity of evolution to others who might not think to ask for it, and allowing them to choose the higher road. Blessing is a way to raise the vibration of every person and situation that you touch or pass — even on the subway platform or to the harried store clerk. This type of activity is what the soul is all about, spreading unconditional love and higher vibrations to all.

A way to make sure you are offering your loving best between blessings is to review your actions. Using the Review Meditation allows you to see what you would like to have done better, and rehearse how you would handle the situation if it comes up again.

CHAPTER 10

The Review Meditation

In all stages of life we are connected with things
that teach us and remind us of who we are.
This day and past days had reminders for each of us,
reminding us of our paths. In a moment of stillness
we can each reflect on our divine role,
connecting to our love. Through that clear vision let
us walk from the fog into the light.

— *DAVID BENNETT, Voyage of Purpose*

The Review Meditation – Lunchtime

1. Take a deep breath and feel your shoulders relaxing as you exhale.
2. Return to breathing normally.
3. Replay the last conversation or action of your day in your mind.
4. Consider that scenario and see if there is something you could have done or said better.
5. If there is, don't beat yourself up. Instead, say to yourself, "I love myself. I will do better next time."
6. Imagine the same situation repeated, but this time respond in a way that better reflects the person you are growing toward being.
7. If you did well in your last conversation or action, then reinforce the experience by imagining yourself reacting the same way in a similar situation.

8. Choose another situation in your day that may provide a key example for improvement or reinforcement and repeat the process.

WHERE AND WHEN

The two best times to do the Review Meditation are after lunch and before you go to sleep. If you have a tendency to obsess over your actions, this meditation can help by allowing you to redo a situation that is bothering you in a way that shows an improvement. Since people don't tend to obsess about what they do right, you will probably find it is the do-overs that you focus on. It is essential to review your positive actions without having an ego party and not judge or beat yourself up over actions you could have done better. Balance is the key here. The Review Meditation helps you access greater mindfulness before you act. In the beginning you will need to go easy on yourself. You are human, and it is human nature not to get it right the first time!

The Review Meditation is also ideal right before you embark on what could be a tricky situation. Remember a time when you acted in a way that helped you accomplish what you wanted and replay that scenario with the upcoming event. If you haven't in the past been able to act the way you want in a similar situation, imagine yourself acting or speaking in the way you'd prefer. Pro golfers use a similar technique when they map out the desired shot in their mind before they strike the ball. You too can practice in your mind how you want to react in any given situation. Practice it, let it go, and allow yourself to do the best you can. Things don't always go the way you plan. Yet, by practicing the Review Meditation on a regular basis you are more likely to be prepared for any situation.

EXAMPLE

I have a habit of tailgating. I don't mean to do it, yet if someone is driving really slowly, you can bet I am up close to that bumper! One day I was driving on a road that I couldn't pass on. I got behind a painfully slow moving Buick. Next thing I knew, I was right up to the car's bumper, almost pushing it to go faster. The Buick slowed down for a right turn, and as the car turned, I saw an older woman driving. Oh no, it's a nun! I went home and told my husband that I almost ran a nun off the road. In my nightly Review Meditation, I thought about what I could have done differently to help me not to tailgate. I came up with a different turn-off I could take that is quicker and would bypass the slow moving car. If I imagine the slow driver as my mother-in-law, who is in her eighties, I will be more patient. I didn't judge myself. Instead I simply imagined the same scenario, picturing the slow-driving nun as my mother-in-law and backing off the tailgating. Then, when the turn comes for the alternate route, I take it.

It has taken more than a few of the same Review Meditations, but I am taking the same route and find myself once again behind a slow-moving car—and right on the car's bumper. I remember this scenario from my Review Meditation, so I begin to think of the driver as my mother-in-law, immediately back off, and give the car plenty of room. I am not in a rush today, so I do not choose to take the alternate route. When the slow car turns off, at the same turn, no less, I see it is a car *full of nuns*! Feeling redeemed and relieved, I know I will have a better Review Meditation tonight!

WHY – KARMA AND SERVICE

My nickname for the Review Meditation is the "Karmic Eraser." I believe that if you learn the lesson you are being sent and continue to show that you learned the lesson during future tests; you have worked through any karma related to the situation. When you see these testing opportunities, think of them as "karma measuring sticks" to show how far you have grown!

Karma is an impersonal Universal Law of cause and effect, used to create balance. You can see karma as an act to balance the Universe. The cause of a particular effect can be an action, a thought, or even a desire. Karma is not "good" or "bad," it is simply a balancing action that creates opportunities for you to continue to evolve.

Karma is not a system of rewards and punishments dictated by a man sitting with a scale to judge your every action. Karma teaches what you need to grow and exist in greater harmony with what is around you. If you think of a nut falling from a tree into a pond, the size of the ripple does not depend on whether it is a good nut or a bad nut; it depends on the force with which the nut hits the water. The strength of your karma is the result of the force of your actions. If you put a lot of force and focus into creating harmony, your karma will reflect that. If you put force into creating *dis*harmony, that too will be reflected in your karma. It isn't that you are being punished for being bad; karma simply applies the amount of force needed to bring you back into harmony with the Universal flow.

An example of this balance is the story of the Guru and the Devotee. The Devotee decides to leave the ashram. The Guru calls him in to question why he is leaving. The Devotee complains that the Guru does not give the same advice to each person. The Devotee is troubled because sometimes the Guru offers conflicting advice. The Guru explained that sometimes a student is going too far to the left of the path and he will tell that student, "Go right! Go to the right," and if a student is veering off the path too far to the right, he tells him, "Move to the left! Go to the left."

Karma is like the Guru, who is simply guiding his students to walk the middle path. Karma guides you into balance with the flow of the Universe; it doesn't judge that left is better than right or up is better than down. The Universal Law of Karma merely brings you into balance.

Karma is often thought of as being from a past life, and as evolution seems to be speeding up, many feel that their karma isn't waiting until their next lifetime to be answered. "Cash karma" is the term used when the opportunity to balance your actions comes soon after you have gotten out of balance. This can be a good thing; it is getting easier to see the correlation between cause and effect. Your opportunity for growth when experiencing this quickened karma is also multiplied.

Because almost every spiritual tradition tells us that karma is balanced by doing service, it brings up the question: Can I help too much? This is a touchy subject in many spiritual circles. I will give you my take on it and leave you to make your own decision. It is natural to feel good about helping others. You are taught that being of service is the best way you can give back. There is truth in this. Service is a major factor to spiritual growth. At the same time, it is also important to make sure that you don't take away someone else's karmic lessons. If karma uses lessons to create balance and evolutionary growth and you take on responsibility of someone's lesson, you can keep that person from learning what he or she needs to learn. You could delay that soul's growth. That is just my opinion. Here is an example:

I had an ex with a temper that came out when he was frustrated. He never took his temper out on me, yet this was an issue he'd had his whole life. He was working hard to bring more spirituality into his life, yet his frustrations and temper sometimes got the best of him. He became frustrated one day, punched a time clock, and hurt his hand pretty badly. It was really sore. Being empathic, I could also feel his pain. I had just come home from healing school where I had learned how to fix things like that. I felt so good that I could take the pain away and so I did. With the pain gone, he pretty much forgot about the situation and the frustration/anger issue he might have had the opportunity to examine. I am sure he had to deal with his frustration and anger again and it probably was a bigger lesson the next time.

What was my role in that? If I hadn't made the hurt go away, he might — I stress *might* — have examined how destructive his temper tantrum was and experienced some growth. I put my need to be a good helper, eliminate his pain, and feel good about myself in front of what was truly best for him. At that moment, I thought I knew what he needed, and in hindsight, I feel I was wrong.

There is a tremendous growth when you are as low as you can be and you play a part in getting yourself back on the right path. I have a friend who will tell you to this day that the best thing to have happened is getting sent to jail in his twenties. It got him back on the right path. When someone never has to deal with the dysfunction of his or her addiction, or whatever issue it is, that person is never given the empowering gift of recovery.

Like with anything, balance is the key. When being a helper, it is important to ask yourself if you are empowering the person to become stronger or if you are enabling that person. The best thing you can do for someone you care about is to empower him or her to not need you anymore. Otherwise a break up is inevitable because one person's growth threatens the unhealthy co-dependent foundation of the relationship. It's like the old saying: "It is better to teach someone to fish rather than fish for them." It is amazing when two people connect as equals in the relationship, instead of because one needs the other. The empowered relationship is more likely to survive in the long run because both can continue to grow and mature.

The important thing is to balance your need to help with knowing the difference between healthy support and a co-dependent reaction. Ask yourself why you are helping. Did the person ask for help? Did you ask the person if he or she wanted help? Is your assistance going to create dependence or independence? I don't think there is a cut-and-dried answer for this situation, but it is something to ponder the next time you get the urge to be of service.

SOUL SOOTHER

Any time you consciously review your actions, you are giving your soul the opportunity to offer input. Through this input, your soul and your guides can help you to see where improvement is needed, and point you in the direction of realizing your potential. By not judging yourself, you are able to look at yourself clearly, without reprimand. This allows you to see yourself truthfully while making adjustments as needed to reinforce what reflects your potential. When you are being of service by empowering others, it does not mean you put your own life on hold. You can be of service to more than one person, and continue to grow and evolve yourself. Your soul wants you to be the best you can be and, if possible, empower others to be the best they can be as well. Being aware of karma allows you to pick up on opportunities your guides give you to balance your karma quickly, bringing your life into equilibrium. When you're not spending time balancing past karma, you can spend more of the present devoted to your evolutionary growth. It does not matter who you have been in the past. Your soul lives in the present moment and offers you a glimpse of your future possibilities when you practice the Review Meditation.

But if you don't want to wait to review your actions after they happen, practicing the Activity Meditation will bring awareness to what you are doing as you do it.

CHAPTER 11

The Activity Meditation

Mindfulness lets us see and notice more detail in every experience. Focus on your five senses of sight, smell, hearing, taste, and touch; it keeps you in this moment. Introduce your sixth sense, of listening to your intuitiveness, let Spirit guide you. Mindfulness can be focused upon anytime during any activity.
— *DAVID BENNETT, Voyage of Purpose*

The Washing Dishes Meditation

1. Take a deep breath and feel your shoulders relaxing as you exhale.
2. Return to breathing normally.
3. Bring your attention to the task in front of you.
4. Focus on doing the dishes, nothing else. Everything else will still be waiting for you when you are done.
5. Be aware as you take the dish in your hands; feel the weight of the dish. Notice if it is heavy or light; notice the color, and the condition.
6. Begin to wash the dish. Feel the temperature of the water on your hands while experiencing the soapiness on your fingers.
7. Sense the texture of the dishrag or sponge.
8. Bring your focus back to your activity if your thoughts stray.
9. Continue to clean the dish, and observe the dish getting cleaner. Run your fingers over the surface — did you get everything?

10. Rinse the dish, sensing the temperature of the water. Feel the water flowing over your hands and onto the dish.
11. Bring your thoughts back to the present moment and your task each time you find yourself thinking of something other than the dishes.
12. Rest the dish in the drying rack and observe the water dripping off the dish. Watch it forming a changing pattern on the drainboard.
13. Repeat the process as you turn to the next dish or glass.

WHERE AND WHEN

How often do we give ourselves the luxury of "single-tasking?" I often wonder how people used to get so many things done. Maybe they didn't try to do so many things at once. Giving a job your undivided attention will ensure that not only is it done right, but it is completed properly the first time! This Activity Meditation can be combined with any activity at any time. Some activities you might want to try this with besides dishwashing are showering, doing laundry, packing, grocery shopping (try picking vegetables to start with), riding a bike, driving (turn the radio and phone off), sewing, talking with a child, cleaning, or making love.

EXAMPLE

Jon dreads when it is time to wash Molly. It is his least favorite chore. Molly, the family dog, is always stressed out at bath time, turning it into a big ordeal. Jon decides to try the Activity Meditation, figuring that washing the dog is like washing dishes except dogs have hair! He gets the tub out of the garage and starts the hose. As with washing the dishes, he focuses on the temperature of the water and notices that it's quite cold. Funny, he never noticed that before. He decides to move the operation inside to the bathtub where he can control the water temperature. Focusing on each step and purposefully releasing his dread, he gets the towels and dog shampoo ready. He double-checks to make sure he has everything he needs. Too often he forgets the towels and then has to struggle to get them before the soaking wet dog shakes off, making a mess that takes even longer to clean up. Knowing he has everything, he remembers to take a deep breath and calmly goes to get Molly. She looks at him warily when he helps her into the tub. Jon once again feels the water, adjusting the temperature. Molly soon knows it is bath time and starts whimpering. This time, instead of Jon getting annoyed with her, he senses her apprehension and starts to talk to her calmly. He slowly lets the water gently touch her back and underbelly. He is surprised she doesn't jump like she usually does. The warmer water and Jon's calming presence is definitely making a difference. Jon continues to slowly wash Molly, while maintaining a calm demeanor and strong focus on the bath process. Before he knows it, he is toweling Molly off, the bathroom isn't a wreck, and they are still best friends!

WHY – INTUITION

As you can see in the example, when Jon practices the Activity Meditation, he becomes more sensitive to Molly's emotions. He is able to calm her down before she gets out of control. Jon may not know it, but his intuition is opening up. Often when you make the effort to become more aware of your surroundings, you also put your intuition "antenna" up. Meditation increases your awareness on all levels, not simply physical. All your senses tend to become more heightened, including the intuitive "sixth sense." How often do you get your best ideas when you are in the shower or driving? At these times, the activity is keeping the mind busy so your intuition can communicate more freely.

When you are meditating, you are more relaxed and less likely to have your mind's stress interfere in your listening. Meditation brings your brainwaves first to the alpha state and then deeper to the theta state. These states are favorable to intuitive knowing. We can easily bypass the conscious mind in the alpha state, and even more so in the theta state. Achieving these deeper states will allow your wiser self to speak with greater freedom and ease.

You can't always be in the alpha or theta state, so intuition is definitely easier when you can tell the difference between your monkey mind-chatter and your wise, intuitive self. As you work on focusing your mind and watching your thoughts with the meditations in *Soul Soothers*, you'll get familiar with your mind's way of communicating. The mind is often judgmental and emotional. The wise self, that is the intuitive part, is remarkably calm and definitely not critical. This is not to say that your intuition always thinks that you are perfect and everyone you know is good for you! Your intuition may tell you that someone is not serving your best interests, yet it will not tell you the person is terrible or out to get you. Think of your intuition as discerning versus judgmental.

You will also find that your intuitive side is not overly dramatic. One time I was in a relationship with a nice man that was not bad, but not going anywhere. While doing a psychic reading for someone else, I advised her that since she wasn't in love with her boyfriend, she needed to think about letting him go so he could find someone who really loved him. She replied that he was a really nice guy and she hated to end the relationship. My guides reminded her that this man deserved someone who really loved him. Then they said to me, "Are you listening?" No drama, just a statement that rang of truth. Such truth, in fact, that I went home and ended our relationship. It was hard at the time, yet I am so glad I heard and honored my intuitive guidance. My ex was engaged to a lovely girl shortly afterward who just adored him, and I went on to marry a man I adore as well.

Intuition comes through in many ways. It is rarely heard out loud like Bill Cosby's "Noah, build me an ark!" That would be *clairaudience*, or clear-hearing. More often you will "hear" clairaudience as an internal voice or as a thought that comes out of nowhere. Intuition is usually direct, unemotional, and not critical. You may also experience a vision of sorts. Most people think they are not good at visualizing, yet if I ask them to picture their front door or a frog, most people can see those images in their mind's eye even with their eyes open. Getting intuition in pictures is called *clairvoyance*, or clear-seeing. An example: I was doing a psychic reading for a woman who asked me about the best nursing home for her mother. I immediately saw a church in my mind's eye. She knew exactly which nursing home I meant, as one looked like a church! There is also *clairsentience*, which is clear-feeling. A common type of clairsentience is psychometry, when you get a strong feeling. *Claircognizance*, or clear-knowing, is when you just know something. You didn't learn it, you were not told it; you just knew it. Think of mother's intuition: this is often claircognizance. Clear-smelling is *clairalience* and *clairgustance* is clear-tasting.

Everyone is different, so be open to the way your intuition comes through. Sometimes intuition can even come through someone else or seem a coincidence. For example, you may find you have been asking for help deciding where to move when you get an invitation to an event in Columbus, Ohio. Is it a coincidence that Columbus was one of your top choices of where to live? Now, not everything is a sign, so honor both your common sense and your intuition when making important decisions.

When you have trouble making decisions, it is important to include what your common sense is telling you along with your intuitive guidance. A practical way to do this is to make a list similar to the "Pros and Cons" list you were probably taught in school. Instead of listing the pros and cons of an option, write what your common sense is telling you on one side and your intuitive guidance on the other. Using both sides, you can ensure you'll take all you need into consideration in order to make a well-rounded and responsible choice.

Pro	Con		Common Sense	Intuition

Many of the exercises in *Soul Soothers* are designed for developing intuition, especially the Breathing, Grounding, and Golden Light Meditations. Yet any meditation where you develop mindfulness and focus as you learn how your mind communicates will help with intuition building. The more you are aware of your mind and environment's influence on your life, the better equipped you will be to hear, see, and know what your intuitive self is offering you.

SOUL SOOTHER

When you allow your mind to focus on just one thing at a time, you sharpen all of your physical senses, such as sight, hearing, touch, smell, and even taste. The sharper your senses, the easier it will be to develop your non-physical sense of clairaudience, clairvoyance, clairsentience, etc. When you are going in the wrong direction, your intuition can clue you in and offer another way to proceed. If doors will not open for you, no matter how much effort you put into a situation, it could be your intuition telling you, "Wrong door!" If you are on the right track, your intuition can help you to stay on track by sending synchronicities and positive reinforcement. The clearer your intuition, the stronger the support and guidance you'll have throughout your day, allowing you to move through life with greater ease and grace.

Yet if you are distracted by noise in your surroundings, you might have trouble hearing your intuition. Choosing the Noise Meditation will allow you to bring your awareness back where it belongs.

CHAPTER 12

The Noise Meditation

How do we center? Better yet, how do we maintain that center?
Through stillness we find our song, our resonant vibration that is
our antenna to universal wisdom. Yet life can knock us off track.
The trick is to recognize it and return to center as best as we can.
With practice and discipline we develop mindful attention and
become centered with increased frequency.

— *DAVID BENNETT, Voyage of Purpose*

The Noise Meditation

1. Take three deep breaths, and with each exhalation, relax
   your shoulders.
2. Return to your regular breathing.
3. Silently say "noise" when you hear the noise you are
   working with.
4. Silently say "quiet," when it stops.
5. Repeat labeling "noise" and "quiet" for a few more cycles.
6. Continue to label the noise each time it occurs.
7. Stop commenting on the quiet. Instead, during the
   quiet, avoid holding onto your thoughts.
8. Allow thoughts to pass by your awareness without placing
   attention or judgment on them. Similar to when you are
   aware of TV commercials yet do not focus on them. Let
   your thoughts become background noise.
9. Continue to label the noise, while allowing thoughts to
   pass by during the quiet time.

10. Discontinue labeling the noise; instead let thoughts about the noise pass, while still letting thoughts go by when the quiet time happens.
11. Be forgiving yet firm when your mind wanders.
12. Let thoughts go by as you expand the space created when sending your thoughts into the background through the rest of your meditation.

WHERE AND WHEN

I developed the "Dog Barking Meditation" when I lived in an apartment with neighbors who had a noisy dog. It is little different than the Noise Meditation: I imagined the barking dog being a monk saying, "*Om*...." I would listen to the *om* and then the silence. Eventually, I was so focused on the silences that the bark/om simply became a way to designate the space between the silences. The Noise Meditation can be used anywhere that it is not silent, which is just about everywhere. This meditation works best with intermittent noises, such as a dog barking or horn beeping.

I do all of my writing at the Creekside Books and Café in our town. The cafe is usually pretty quiet, although it can get noisy at lunchtime. I can even hear people talking when I have my headphones on. There are not enough breaks in the sounds to do the traditional Noise Meditation. But by not paying attention to the words being spoken, I turn the nonstop voices into a background hum. I keep my focus on the music coming through my headphones and my writing, and after a few minutes, even my music becomes background noise. The result is that there is nothing in my awareness other than my writing.

Another way to deal with unpleasant noises or vibrations is to practice the "Atomizer Meditation." If you have tried the Noise Meditation and it hasn't helped enough, imagine yourself becoming separate molecules, like in *Star Trek* when they beam up Captain Kirk. Allow the sounds or vibrations to pass right through the spaces between your molecules without affecting you. When you no longer feel the undesirable effect, start to beam yourself back into solidity. It is best to do a quick Grounding Meditation after this to make sure you are reconnected to the Earth.

EXAMPLE

Max is trying to get to sleep, but the traffic outside his brother's apartment is so loud that it is stressing him out. Every time the light changes, the cars rev their engines right under his window. He decides to try the Noise Meditation. He hasn't done this one yet because noise isn't really an issue where he lives. The light changes and he hears the cars start to rev. He imagines a group of drummers playing music outside in the street. His brain tells him they are cars, but he goes with the image anyway. The revving stops and he starts to be aware of the lower noise level and silently says "quiet." The light changes to green, and the accelerating cars startle Max once again. Instead of getting tense, he sees this as the end of the quiet phase and back into the *music* stage, so he says "*music*." As Max goes back and forth between "quiet" and "*music*," he realizes there is a comforting rhythm. He starts to hear it all as a sort of white noise sound and starts to label the revving motors as "sound" and the relative quiet as "sound." He is no longer jolted every time the light changes and soon Max is drifting off to sleep.

WHY – THE VIBRATION EFFECT

Do you ever wonder why noise like a car honking or the ballast hum of those long florescent light bulbs bothers you? You will need to understand a few concepts about vibration. Everything vibrates. At a molecular level, even the chair you are sitting on is vibrating. Metaphysicians understood this long before science figured it out.

Vibrations can be thought of as waveforms. Like a wave on the ocean, each vibration has a swell and a dip. Each set of swells and dips can be measured, and that measurement becomes its frequency. Say it is a stormy night and the swells and dips come quickly; this would be thought of, in our analogy, as a faster and higher frequency.

FREQUENCY OF SOUND WAVES

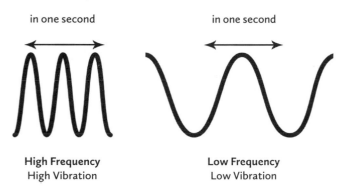

in one second · in one second

High Frequency
High Vibration

Low Frequency
Low Vibration

Rhythm entrainment, more simply called sympathetic vibration or resonance, is when two waveforms of similar frequency and phase lock together. The waves swell and dip at the same time. This sympathetic resonance creates increased amplitude. Think of this as two radios in the house, tuned to the same station, sounding louder than if each were playing different stations. Two similar vibrations get stronger when they are put together.

The last concept you will find helpful is that of *entrainment*. If two vibrations are next to each other long enough, the weaker vibration will tend to start to adjust its vibration to match the stronger vibration.

AMPLIFIED WAVE

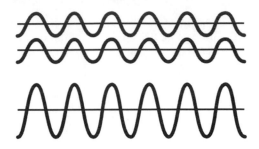

Amplified wave from two similar waves

ENTRAINMENT

The vibrations of two people influence each other

two people with different vibrations meet

the stronger vibration (bold) remains the same,
the weaker one (light) remains weaker but is raised
through the encounter with the stronger one

An example of vibration change is found when looking at ice, water, and steam. Temperature can be seen as a change in vibration. One difference between ice, water, and steam is its level of vibration. The ice is vibrating at a low level and the steam is vibrating at a high one.

If you surround an ice cube (low vibration) with steam (high vibration), its vibration will rise and the ice starts to melt. As the temperature raises it first becomes water (medium vibration) on its way to steam. We are all vibrating and, like the ice, another vibration can affect our rate of vibration and even our physical being.

You can feel the vibration of music as well. Some music might soothe your soul while another person's favorite song makes you tense. You may find that you like different music depending on the mood you are in. You can think of your mood as a reflection of your vibration. I definitely do not vibrate at the same level as the ballast in our closet's florescent light. My mood is one of agitation if my husband leaves the closet light on, even if I can't hear or see it. If I am not being mindful, I get grumpy and don't know why. If I am aware enough of my body, I will feel merely uncomfortable. But if I am really mindful, I will walk over to the closet, find the light on, turn it off, and all is okay with the world again!

People have this vibratory effect on you too. There might not be anything outwardly wrong with a person, but you just don't like being around him or her. The person's vibration might not fit with yours. It's discordant and both of you will feel uncomfortable. The stronger person's vibration will start to pull on the weaker person's vibration and start to shift the weaker one. On the other hand, when two people are around each other with similar energy, the matching vibrations are amplified or strengthened. This is how mob mentality comes about. The more energies vibrating at a similar level, the stronger the vibration becomes. A person may be in a great mood. Yet coming into an angry crowd, the amplified angry vibration will overpower his or her normal positive vibration, turning the person angry like the crowd. This works the opposite way as well. Someone who is grumpy may come to a relaxed spa environment and little by little the person relaxes to match the vibration of the spa.

Vibrations can have the same effect in relationships. If you are evolving more quickly, or your vibration is higher than your mate's, the contrasting vibrations can annoy both of you. Especially when both of you are comfortable where you are in life. A woman's mate may feel like she is trying to change him. He may not even know why he is angry or why being home, around her, feels uncomfortable. On the other hand, being around him may bring her energy and vibration down. If she is not mindful of her energy, she could feel depressed when around her mate, thinking it is the relationship, when it is simply a conflict between two discordant vibrations. If you are aware of your vibration — how yours affects your mate and how his or hers affects yours — you can lessen the struggle. Trying to force someone to evolve or vibrate at a different level will simply create conflict. It is more effective to continue on your path and be a shining example, demonstrating how a positive outlook and compassion can make for a happier life. As it is said, you can lead a horse to water, but you can't make it drink. You can try to force your mate to follow your path, but you are more likely to end up with a cranky mate.

This is why being consciously aware of your vibration and the vibration of the environment you are in is so important. If you consciously vibrate at a positive and loving vibration, you are more likely to create a positive environment around you or trigger the opportunity for the change needed to make it so. This is why a person who is growing spiritually suddenly finds his or her life filled with chaos. He or she is seeing the result of vibrational shifts.

The key words here are *consciously vibrate*. Vibrations are strongly affected by will. When you go into a situation choosing to be positive, it will be much harder for another's negativity to bring you down. If you are not conscious of your vibration, you will feel much better having lunch with Positive Polly than Negative Nellie, because your energy won't be unconsciously lowered. When you are consciously staying positive, Negative Nellie doesn't stand a chance and may not want to have lunch again. A win-win! I find the quickest way to deal with a complaining companion is to ask, "Well, what are you going to do about it?" Vibrate at as high a level you can by staying as positive as possible. Yet a word of advice: manipulation will only send out manipulative energy, so use this technique with only the most loving intentions, always asking that your vibration affects others in ways that are for the highest and most loving good of all those concerned.

So the good news is that you are not stuck with a certain vibration around you or within you. You can either tune it out with the Noise Meditation, shift the energy with a Blessing Meditation, or use one of the meditations coming up to consciously adjust your "dial" to compensate for your own vibration.

SOUL SOOTHER

Understanding the Universal Law of Vibration allows you to be in control of your own energy and, used consciously, positively affect your environment. This is a huge responsibility, yet the reward is massive. When you are aware of how vibrations affect you, you can make a conscious choice whether or not to stay in an environment where you have to struggle to maintain your level of vibration. You will also be able to tell when you are in a place that sustains or even assists you to raise your vibrational rate even higher. Most important, through conscious awareness of your own vibration, you can become a beacon of positive energy where ever you go.

Understanding the interconnection that allows you to affect your surroundings is enhanced when you practice the Observation Meditation in the next chapter.

CHAPTER 13

The Observation Meditation

We all walk on our individual paths, many times in the dark and feeling alone. Yes, they are our individual pathways, but with the awakening of more people around the globe we find more paths running parallel and crisscrossing. Let's shine our lights so others may see our paths are next to theirs.

— *DAVID BENNETT, Voyage of Purpose*

The Observation Meditation

1. Choose something to observe, like a group of people.
2. Take three deep breaths, and with each exhalation, experience your shoulders relax.
3. Return to breathing normally.
4. Start to watch the people as a group. Avoid focusing on one person.
5. Notice where they are walking. Is there anything in their path? Are they all walking the same direction? If not, focus on those walking in one direction.
6. Ask yourself these questions: Are the people walking at the same pace? Do they appear aware of the others walking along with them? Do they seem to be walking as one big group or a bunch of individuals?
7. Let thoughts and judgments flow through without paying attention to them. People are not good or bad — they are merely human beings.

8. Return to observing.
9. Be sensitive to the flow of the group rather than any one individual. What happens when the group comes to a corner or intersection? Do the people flow seamlessly or do they stop suddenly? Do they seem to be aware of anything going on in their surroundings, or with one another? What changes affect them?
10. Open up your focus even wider. Notice the entire group's traffic pattern. Do the people walking in the other direction affect the group you have been observing?
11. Notice if outside noises or added people cause a break in the group's flow?
12. To take your observation further, move to another area and another group of people.
13. Look to see if these people are creating similar or different patterns.

WHERE AND WHEN

The Observation Meditation is best done in nature, traffic, or with crowds of people. It is not polite to observe one person in the detail you need for this meditation. In nature, squirrels are perfect for this technique. You can see how the environment affects the squirrel as much as its own inquisitive nature. As in the meditation above, you can look to see how physical barriers, sounds, other people, store-fronts, signs, and even energy affect how people move and react. If you are near a road, you can watch traffic. How does one aggressive driver affect the actions of others? I would not try the Observation Meditation while you are driving; yet if you have a bird's-eye view of an intersection or highway, watching traffic can be a lesson in human behavior. Eventually you will find your awareness opening up to the surroundings of what you are watching. When in nature, you will find that you start to become part of the ecosystem rather than an observer of it.

EXAMPLE

Kiki is sitting at the mall, waiting for her husband, Tim, to join her for a quick dinner before they head home. She finishes checking her email and decides to use the time before her husband arrives to try the Observation Meditation. Kiki chooses a seat at an intersection with a kiosk that has a young woman hawking body lotion. As she watches the traffic pattern of the people walking by, she first notices that there are two types of people at the mall today. There are the "lookers" who are taking their time contemplating each store window to see if there is anything that interests them and the "shoppers on a mission": who stare straight ahead and don't look at the windows at all. The shoppers on a mission walk faster than the lookers and seem more tense and focused. Kiki can feel the stress when the mission shoppers go by, noticing that her breathing is shallower when she focuses on them. When she switches to the lookers, she feels her shoulders relax and she breathes more deeply. Thinking about how energy and vibrations travel, she realizes how different types of shoppers affect her, even though she is sitting at a distance, simply observing. Her attention is drawn to the shoppers as they encounter the hawker selling hand lotion. The traffic pattern shifts altogether when the shoppers notice the kiosk. The response of the shoppers is almost as if the kiosk were infected. Kiki catches her attention drifting to her husband's whereabouts, so she returns to observing. Most of the shoppers change their traffic pattern to walk around the kiosk, keeping as far away as possible. Some of the mission shoppers are so focused on their destination that they don't even notice the young woman trying to get their attention. The majority of the shoppers say, "No thank you." The mission shoppers tend to have a scowling response, whereas the lookers seem more relaxed and less annoyed. A few of the lookers even stop to try a dab. The hawker isn't having much luck until a stressed-out mom pushing a double stroller starts to walk by and then — Kiki could almost see the wheels turning in the mother's head — changes her mind and returns to the kiosk. The mother lets the young woman gently massage the body lotion into her hand. The hawker sees how stressed the mom is and even gifts her with a free little sample. Kiki can literally feel the mother's stress melt away as she accepts the gift and moves on to her errands. Kiki remembers how stressed she sometimes got when she had young children and is reminded how important it is, even now, to allow a minute of relaxation when she is overworked. Tim arrives right on time, but looking a little stressed. Kiki takes a minute to give him a hug, watches his shoulders relax, and they go off to dinner.

WHY – INTERCONNECTION

The Observation Meditation allows you to connect to the world around you in a deeper way than available to you when you are interacting. The first thing you usually notice when observing, like Kiki did, is that you'll start to feel similar to the environment you are watching. Once you are conscious of this, you can either choose to stay with that feeling or make a conscious effort to return to your own vibration. If you are observing nature and find it relaxing, you may want to allow your vibration to start to match the one you are experiencing. If it is stressful, like connecting with the mission shoppers, you may choose to refocus on your own vibration so you don't get caught up in theirs.

Once you realize that you are affected by other vibratory rates, you'll become highly aware of the importance of maintaining a positive vibration. This is especially true now, since many people are not conscious enough to affect their own vibrations.

The fact that one person's vibration can co-mingle with your own shows your interconnectedness with everything around you. It is through knowing that you are interconnected with everyone and everything that brings up a second understanding that comes from the Observation Meditation. What you do to your neighbor you are also doing to yourself. How does that work? Assume you and your neighbor are arguing about him planting a tree on your mutual property line. If you do something mean, like cut down the disputed tree, it will cause him anguish. If he is vibrating anguish, it will affect you and your energy field, causing you to carry a vibration of anguish. Also, if he is constantly thinking negatively about you, remembering that energy flows where attention goes, you are being bombarded with discordant energy. This does not mean you cannot protect yourself by keeping your energy higher than your neighbor's. Yet if you do something like cut down your neighbor's tree in anger, your energy is probably not very high and you are more likely to be adversely affected. Remember that all of creation is made up of the same energy, at varying levels of vibration. You and the angry neighbor are made up of the same essence. It is as if you both are made from the same batch of cookie dough, yet one of you is decorated with blue sprinkles and the other with mini M&M's. The dough is your shared essence and the toppings in this cookie analogy relate to your vibratory rates. What makes you different from another person, or even the chair you are sitting on, is your vibratory rate. This not only works when someone is nearby: the vibrations you put forth will affect the entire planet.

Your intention, whether in word, thought, or deed, will affect the vibrations and energy around you and thereby affect you. You cannot get away from this interconnectedness. The healthiest choice you have is to be mindful of your own vibrations, its well-being, and how it affects your surroundings. You can choose to take the high road and be the high vibration in any given situation, or you can choose to muck around by adding to the lower vibrations you are presented with. You can be a positive influence in your world. Think of a snowball fight. If the snowballs represent negative thoughts, every time you throw a snowball, you are giving the other person more negative energy to throw back at you. Or you can think of positive thoughts as flames, two flames put together can increase and strengthen the amount of light each flame could cast on its own. Through consciously choosing to be positive, you can raise the vibrations of your world through your interconnection with it.

SOUL SOOTHER

Understanding your interconnection empowers you to take responsibility for your energy and the effect you have on your environment. Remember how a stronger vibration creates a shift in the lower vibration, and you'll see why the best thing you can do, not only for yourself but also for humanity and the world, is to be conscious of your vibratory rate. By using the tools already discussed, taking time for yourself, breathing deeply, being grounded, maintaining awareness of how your energy affects others, staying mindful, refraining from judging, being grateful, understanding karma, taking time to contemplate, using your intuition, and being aware of your vibration, you can be a strong and powerful creator using your interconnectedness with all things to assist in raising the vibrations of your environment and the world. A world without differing vibrations is not the goal, as individuality is one reason you came here. Yet a world where everyone is aware of their interconnection, and vibrating at their highest level, would result in a world filled with people who are more compassionate, aware of consequences, grounded, mindful, discerning, as well as responsible for their own actions and subsequent vibratory level. You can be the start of a domino effect of shifting vibrations. Being conscious of how your vibrations affects others allows you to choose what type of world you live in.

A wonderful way to shift your vibration is through the Mantra Meditation.

CHAPTER 14

The Mantra Meditation

Love is the unifying language of the universe. The glue that brings together the vibratory atoms into this mass we know as you and I. If there is one thing our ego mind has to grasp onto in this life, let it be Love.

— *DAVID BENNETT, Voyage of Purpose*

The Mantra Meditation

1. Choose a positive word or phrase. For example, "I am brave" rather than "I am not fearful."
2. Once you have your word or phrase, take a few deep breaths to start the meditation.
3. Return to breathing normally.
4. Silently repeat your word or phrase over and over again for about 30 seconds.
5. Allow thoughts to come in; let them pass without attention and go back to repeating your word or phrase.
6. Continue repeating your word or phrase until you have achieved the desired shift.
7. Take your Mantra Meditation a step further; use a mala (prayer beads), or bracelet or necklace with beads. As you say your word or phrase, count off one bead. This is similar to saying the rosary.

WHERE AND WHEN

I like the Mantra Meditation for right after work. It creates a sacred space in a hectic day and reminds me that right now is a fresh, new moment. Similar to saying grace before dinner, the Mantra Meditation reminds you to set your intention for what comes next. A mantra can also help when your mind won't get off a particular thought or worry. Make sure that you are selecting a word or phrase that feels good to you. I prefer "I am loved," when I am feeling out of sorts and use the word "Release" when I have trouble with obsessing. It might take you a couple of rounds, but you can usually succeed in letting go of those nagging thoughts after only a few repetitions. You might want to use a mala, bracelet, or necklace to count your word or phrase. A mala is a string of prayer beads. Eastern malas have 108 beads, whereas Islamic malas have 99 beads. Those popular "power bead" bracelets usually have 27 beads. Depending on how many times you want to say your mantra, keep going around the mala, bracelet, or necklace.

When you need to make a quick decision, a mantra can help you to refocus enough to think clearly. If you are about to lose your temper, a quick mantra of "Calm" can get your emotions back into control. I find the mantra "Cooperation" works well when I want to create a vibration of cooperation around me. For example, I use this when I have to make a return to a store without my receipt. Yet, remember that manipulation will create the vibration of manipulation around you. If you find yourself judging someone or a situation, a quick mantra of "Loving intent" can wipe those judgments away. Anywhere you feel the need to create a sacred moment, or want to change your mindset, the Mantra Meditation will do the trick. Make sure to use a positive statement, as there are power and energy to words.

EXAMPLE

Kathy and Greg are having a tough go of it lately. They constantly find fault with each other and nitpick. At dinner, Greg picks on the way Kathy sets the table. Greg's family always puts the knife, fork, and spoon together on one side. Kathy sets the table the way her family does. The fork goes to the left and the knife and spoon go on the right. She is so frustrated with Greg's picking on her that she is about to say something snarky. Kathy remembers that the Mantra Meditation is great for changing mindsets and so chooses the word "Cooperation." She takes a quick walk around the living room to repeat her mantra. By the time she gets back to the kitchen, she is calm and able to have a serious talk with Greg about their recent troubles. Kathy takes responsibility for her own nitpicking, admits she really cares for him, and asks that they both stop finding fault and start talking about their real issues.

WHY – THE POWER OF SOUND AND WORD

The word mantra comes from the root *manas* and *trai*. The first means "mind" and the latter means "to free." From this we can see that a mantra is meant to "free the mind." You can look to the mantra to help free yourself from mind-chatter and thoughts. Mantras use a positive word or phrase in order to shift your vibration and consciousness. Words, whether spoken aloud or not, have a vibration. Add *intention* to the word and together they create a powerful force. As discussed in the last chapter, everything in the world is vibrating. Thought or spoken aloud, words are made up of sounds. Sounds create and send forth a vibration.

This relationship of creation and sound is demonstrated in a number of spiritual traditions. It is found in the Creation myth of Christianity's Gospel of John: "In the beginning was the Word. And the Word was with God and the Word was God ..." Another reference is found in the Hindu Vedas where it is said that humanity's essence is speech, and that ideas are not made manifest except through speech. Even the Dali Lama in *The Kalachakra Tantra* declares that without the mantra, one could not attain Buddhahood. Creating a universe or Buddhahood may not be your goal today, yet these traditions speak to the importance of word, sound, and creation.

Words have different sound vibrations and frequencies. Both Ernst Chladni a eighteenth century German physicist and musician and Dr. Hans Jenny, a physician and natural scientist in the 1960s, found that different sound vibrations made distinctive, and sometimes beautiful, patterns in sand. Another researcher, Dr. Masaru Emoto, author of *Messages from Water,* found that words projected onto water can actually change the cells of the water. Positive words tended to create beautiful cellular structures whereas angry words created a discordant cell structure. Since your body is 70 percent water, Dr. Emoto's work could well have groundbreaking consequences. Imagine how using a mantra of positive words with high frequencies will affect you, even down to the cellular level!

You don't have to be a scientist to see the effect of words and their vibrations. Try this simple experiment on your own. Say to yourself, or aloud, the words *despair* and *hate*. How do you feel? You most likely don't feel good and might even feel your energy level sink. Now say "joy" and "love." Feel how those words can actually pick you up and improve your mood. Joy and love clearly have a higher frequency or vibration than the first set!

If you are still wondering if sounds and words can really affect physical objects, think of how the opera singer can use the frequency of her voice to break glass. Or how you can tell if someone is saying angry words in a foreign language, even if you are listening from another room. Mantras can use the vibration of the word to affect you emotionally, mentally, and even, as Dr. Emoto has shown, cellularly.

Remembering that the word *mantra* comes from a combination of words meaning "freeing the mind," know that the mantra can also be used to quiet the mind. There is a wonderful story about an elephant walking in a parade. The elephant would always take the melons from the vendors on the side of the parade route. So, the elephant's keeper gave the elephant a stick to hold on to with his trunk. The stick kept the elephant's trunk busy and full so that he wouldn't grab the fruit. A mantra is like the stick, and our mind is like the elephant. A mantra keeps the mind occupied so that it is not looking for more "food" and goes only where we tell it to!

Similar to our example, you can use a mantra to focus your mind on what you want instead of what your mind chooses to obsess about. Because words have vibration, it is so important to choose your mantra carefully. Use positive words; instead of focusing on what you don't want, choose words that express what you do want. Always say a mantra using the positive form. This goes for affirmations as well.

Affirmations are used to challenge destructive beliefs and strengthen positive ones. By choosing positive beliefs to reinforce, an affirmation is telling the mind what to believe. The mind has to either rework any beliefs that contradict the affirmation or totally deny the affirmation. It is common for people to affirm what they want in order for the mind to let go of limiting beliefs that might otherwise interfere with attaining goals. It is important, just as in the mantra, to use positive statements. For example, "I am not poor," is better expressed as "I am fulfilled." You would not necessarily use "I am rich," because "rich" has a mixed connotation. If you want money, yet resent those who are rich, you may find that saying "I am rich" could carry an unintended resentful vibration. When you think of the word *fulfilled*, you think of a positive version of someone who has what he or she wants in life. It may be financial, yet it also may be fulfilled in love, work, and lifestyle. There is a story, which may be true or not, of a woman who kept affirming that she will receive one hundred thousand dollars. She did get it: her husband passed away and the life insurance was one hundred thousand dollars. The moral of the story is that it is fine to affirm things, yet always intend that whatever you receive must be for the highest and most loving good for all those concerned. When you are mindful of how the words you speak to yourself, and others, creates vibrations that make real change, you can use your words to create, re-tune, and transform your consciousness, and consequently, the world around you.

SOUL SOOTHER

Obsessing about something you have no control over, or getting so caught up in your life that you lose your center, creates physical, emotional, and mental stress. This lack of awareness can even limit you on a soul level. It is very difficult for your soul, guides, and angels to reach you when you are obsessing or on automatic pilot. When you give yourself the opportunity to break out of a destructive pattern long enough to re-center, your soul can then interact with you more easily. You will be able to sense all the guidance offered from higher realms, even if you cannot actually hear the instructions. The Mantra Meditation allows you to create a sacred space in the middle of even the most hectic day. Using mantras and affirmations, you can set your intention for a more positive outlook. Both allow you to take a spiritual break to release, re-center, and re-focus on more than your next errand.

When you learn to create a sacred moment for yourself, you can take advantage of the Contemplation Meditation, which will double your ability to bring yourself back to mindful awareness and bring in the guidance necessary to move forward on your soul's goals as well as your to-do list.

CHAPTER 15

The Contemplation Meditation

Life is so like flowing water, ever moving forward and changing. We can learn a lot from water. You cannot grasp it without it slipping through your fingers. It follows the path of least resistance and wears down obstacles in the path. Oh if we could flow down our true paths.

— *DAVID BENNETT, Voyage of Purpose*

The Three-Minute Contemplation Meditation

1. Acquire a three-minute, hourglass-style egg timer.
2. Get a pen and paper ready for after you've finished your contemplation.
3. Choose a thought, issue, or even a situation in your day that is troubling you. Pick something spiritually oriented like universal love or something practical like how to handle the co-worker wearing strong perfume at work.
4. Take out your egg timer and place it on your desk, table, or countertop. You should be able to comfortably watch the sand flowing from the top to the bottom.
5. Take three deep breaths, and with each exhalation, experience your shoulders relaxing.
6. Return to breathing normally.
7. Watch the sand flow from the top of the hourglass to the bottom, and keep your thoughts focused on the sand falling.

8. Go back to observing the sand falling when your mind interrupts, which it will. Be aware how your thoughts interrupting create a dual focus.

9. Once you are able to focus on the sand without your mind creating distractions, allow the dual focus to return as you keep watching the sand and at the same time think about your chosen contemplation. You may feel a slight shift in your mind as you allow this dual focus to continue.

10. Release any worries that you will forget what comes to you during this exercise. Simply allow your mind to contemplate your issue and watch the sand.

11. Jot down your thoughts on the paper after you are done. Or, if you don't have time, simply go back to your day with the stronger focus and calm you developed during this meditation.

WHERE AND WHEN

You can use the Contemplation Meditation to help you clear your mind by watching the sand fall for just a few seconds or you can use it for problem solving by focusing all your attention on a particular problem. If you watch the whole flow process, your meditation will take three minutes. If you don't have three minutes, you can stop at any time. Using this meditation with a short meaningful passage will allow you to bring the vibration of the passage into your day. You can do this meditation sitting at your desk at work. An egg timer simply looks like a mini-hourglass rather than a meditation tool. You can buy one online or at your favorite kitchen store. I bought one of mine at Wal-Mart and the other at Rhubarb Kitchen & Garden Shop, a quaint kitchen shop in my village, for about four dollars. Most people will think it is a decoration.

The Contemplation Meditation can also be used before you drive home from work, a doctor's appointment, or shopping. Keep the hourglass in your car, briefcase, or purse. Sit it on your dash, or simply hold it while you do a quick Contemplation Meditation before you run your errands. Try this Contemplation Meditation when you need to focus your ideas or figure out what you want to say to someone before you speak to him or her. If you choose a spiritual passage to contemplate, this meditation can be a wonderful way to surround yourself with a positive vibration. When you contemplate a spiritual idea, you bring that vibration into your energy field. Choose a short phrase like "Universal Love," or pick just one line of a meaningful passage so you don't have to look at the words.

EXAMPLE

Annie is having trouble with her new roommate, Margaret. She wants to make this arrangement work, but Margaret has a habit of not cleaning up after herself in the kitchen until the morning. Today, Annie found ants all over the kitchen table. After cleaning the ants up, disinfecting the table, washing Margaret's dishes, and putting out ant traps, Annie is ready to ask her to leave. Knowing that is not the solution, she decides to use this problem as her Contemplation Meditation.

Pulling out her egg timer, she sets it on the (now clean) kitchen table. First Annie simply watches the sand flow from the top of the hourglass down to the bottom. She can smell the cleaning solution on her fingers and starts thinking about getting hand cream. She realizes her thoughts have gone astray and gently brings them back to the sand. When she successfully watches the sand for about 30 seconds, she starts to think about Margaret. She thinks about how nice it has been to have Margaret around, to have someone to say hello to in the morning and watch TV with, and how Margaret respects when Annie wants the living room to herself. Then Annie thinks how helpful the extra money has been. She has had money left over at the end of the month instead of stressing like she used to. The sand finishes its descent, so Annie turns the timer over. All in all, Margaret is a positive addition to the house. Margaret even feeds Annie's cats when she travels to visit her parents. Annie goes back to watching the sand and suddenly gets the inspiration to ask Margaret if they could take turns cleaning the kitchen. Whoever's night it is, will clean the dishes, wipe off the table, and sweep the floor. She'll mention, in a lighthearted manner, that it would be great if this could be done before bedtime so that the ants don't decide to have their own dinner party. Feeling better, and noticing this one took an extra turn of the hourglass, Annie feels it was a good six minutes spent and goes off to find her hand lotion.

WHY – CONTEMPLATION

Contemplation and meditation are often thought of as the same thing, yet contemplation is a form of meditation that allows you to quiet your mind and focus on what you want to gain wisdom about. It also allows your mind to understand that you aren't trying to cut it out of the picture totally. You are acknowledging your mind's value while, in the case of the Three-Minute Meditation, giving it boundaries in which to operate.

Boundaries allow the mind to be stronger and better equipped to use all of its senses, including intuition. Most of the meditations you have been practicing in *Soul Soothers* have been focused on quieting the mind. Contemplation teaches the mind a healthy, active way of interacting. Contemplation also allows you to focus, as with a mantra, on a word or phrase. Yet, unlike the mantra, the mind is allowed to work along with intuition to bring ideas and wisdom from your guides, angels, and soul.

Contemplation is comparable to the game where you start the sentence and someone else has to finish it. Yet here you provide your higher guidance with the topic you want to contemplate, and in turn your guidance can relay the information from which you will benefit. The mind, by focusing on the sand, creates a soft focus and this softer focus allows it to engage yet not control. This idea of the mind having a softer focus is similar to how you benefit when adapting a softer focus when dealing with a difficult person. Similarly, through softening the focus of your mind by watching the sand, you relax your mind's entanglement with the spiritual theme or problem you are contemplating. Psychics also use this softening technique. I have a tendency to look off into the distance or into a crystal when I am listening to my guides. This allows me to disengage from the client's hopes or fears, as well as my own mind's opinions, in a way that I can clearly receive my guide's impartial guidance.

Impartiality is one of the main reasons you only want your mind to *process* the higher guidance, not try to think of a solution on its own. Some of the most helpful information I offer clients comes when I have no idea what I am talking about, but they do!

The important thing is not that I understand, but that I simply relay what my guides are telling me. Your mind has lots of opinions, prejudices, fears, and hopes. Through allowing the mind to be involved, yet not fully engaged, you bring in your higher guidance while your mind processes the information in a way that you can practically apply it to improve your life.

SOUL SOOTHER

Your soul has so much to share with you. Think of your soul as your divine life preserver and instruction manual that you bring with you when you incarnate. Your soul has all the information you will need to complete what you want to accomplish here. Life will present you with the experience and opportunity to grow; yet your soul has all that you need to succeed. Contemplation, and meditation in general, allows you clearer access to your soul that in turn helps you to have access to all that information you brought with you. Your soul is also your connection to your Higher Self, Soul Group, and the rest of your Divine Light. The more you do to teach the mind to give up enough control to work with these higher energies, the more prepared you will be to accept, succeed, and enjoy all of life's challenges and rewards. Yet, with a poor attitude, it is hard to make use of even the best advice.

Using the Attitude Adjuster Meditation in the next chapter will allow you the best headspace to work with your guidance.

CHAPTER 16

The Attitude Adjuster Meditation

In this physical life we learn everything has
a duality, everything has its pair of opposites.
Opposite poles are really only the two extremes
of the same thing with varying degrees between
them. In the light everything is complete yet at
the same time a part of the whole or Oneness
existing in multiple dimensions. You can see how
these two views can differ in how one lives life.

— *DAVID BENNETT, Voyage of Purpose*

The Attitude Adjuster Meditation

1. Take three deep breaths, relaxing your shoulders with each exhalation.
2. Return to breathing normally.
3. Take a moment to observe what your mood is right now. Are you relaxed, tired, hyper?
4. If you are tired, remember a time when you were energized. How did that feel?
5. If you are feeling hyper, remember a time that you were feeling relaxed. How did that feel?
6. Label these memories of how you felt at different times, along with how you feel in the present moment, as your "Energy Level."

7. Close your eyes, if you wish to do so. Yet this exercise can also be done with eyes open.
8. Imagine a dial, like the dial on your stove, yet with degrees of Energy Level on it. This dial has "Tired" at one end, in the middle is "Rested" and at the far end, it reads "Energized."
9. Taking note of how you are feeling right now. Where is your dial set?
10. If you like where you are, there is no need to tweak your dial.
11. Shift your energy level by using your memory of what the different settings feel like.
12. Start turning the dial, allowing yourself to feel your Energy Level shift as the dial moves.
13. Hold onto that adjusted feeling and continue to feel your adjusted Energy Level as you open your eyes and return to your day.

WHERE AND WHEN

The Attitude Adjuster can be done anytime and anywhere, yet it is most helpful when you first become aware that you are not in the headspace you want to be. Often it is difficult to will yourself to have a different outlook, yet when you can remember how it felt to be in a different mindset, you can consciously slide to your desired level for an easier transition. You don't want to be at either extreme of the dial. Yet you can tweak your energy level, mood, emotions, and even your patience by creating a dial for your needs and remembering what it felt like in the past to be at each setting of the dial.

Although closing your eyes will reduce distraction, you don't have to, so you can do this meditation sitting at work, dealing with an annoying person, or standing in line at the grocery store. The Attitude Adjuster can be used when you are in traffic, dealing with a troublesome relative, and even when going on a romantic date.

Your energy or headspace doesn't have to be bad. Some people have trouble going back to work after a vacation or taking "me" time after putting the kids to bed. You can create a dial for whatever you want to shift to and use it to change your attitude, energy, and vibration.

EXAMPLE

Somehow, Pax has lost the calming effect from her Walking Meditation as she enters the store to get the security tag removed from the pants she bought last night. She starts thinking of all the things she could be doing instead of going back to the mall today. Standing in line at Customer Service, she opens her wallet to get out the receipt in case they need to see it. Since opening her wallet is one of her mindfulness bells, Pax silently says, "Bell," and begins to check her state of mind. She realizes that her cranky mindset and energy vibration are not going to make this any easier, so Pax decides to try the Attitude Adjuster Meditation. She thinks of how excited and happy she felt when she found these pants last night and decides that "excited and happy" energy is how she wants to vibrate now. She imagines her Energy Level dial, noticing she is pretty high on the cranky side. Smiling to herself and remembering that excited and happy feeling, she slowly starts to turn the dial to the excited and happy mood she wants to be in. Thinking about the feeling of finding the perfect pants brings her to a better headspace. She is now next in line and walks up to the counter smiling. The woman behind the desk lets out a sigh of relief. She has a sick child at home, is having a tough day at work, and the next angry customer is going to do her in! She and Pax laugh as they talk about how difficult people make life so much more challenging. Pax remarks on how much easier it is to smile than frown. The lady behind the counter smiles back, apologizes again for the trouble, wishes her a great day, and Pax decides that having to come back wasn't so much trouble after all.

WHY – UNIVERSAL LAW OF POLARITY

Taking a minute or two to adjust your headspace can bring you back to your center, clear your mind, and allow you to respond to life the way you want to rather than in a knee-jerk reactive way. But how does the Attitude Adjuster Meditation work? Think about how to get the shower to the perfect temperature. You feel the temperature of the water and if it is too hot, you add some cold. If it is too cold, you add hot. Although your tap only gives you hot and cold water, by using different amounts of each, you get the perfect warm. It is the same way with vibrations.

Adjusting any type of vibration uses the Law of Polarity. You already learned through the Law of Vibration that everything vibrates. The Law of Polarity teaches that everything has an opposite. These opposites can be seen as different levels or degrees of vibration. Even Spirit and matter are different only in their level of vibration. All manifestations are different only in their level of vibration, so changing the level of vibration will change what is manifested. Changing your mindset is accomplished by slowly adjusting your mood vibration toward the desired vibration along the pole of "Mood." To explain this using the example of "Temperature," imagine a curtain rod with the slower vibration, "Cold," at one end. At the other end of the rod is the opposite manifestation, the quicker vibration, which in this example, would be "Hot." As you move up and down the pole of temperature, you start to move into "Warm" or "Cool." If you are running too hot, add some cold to the mix and you will get cooler. You could just as easily use "Liberal" and "Conservative" on the pole of "Political Ideology" or "Black," "Gray," and "White" on the pole of "Grayscale."

POLE OF TEMPERATURE

Hot   Warm   Cool   Cold

It is a matter of recognizing that all emotional and mental states, even moods or ideologies, are different only as matter of degree. You can raise and lower the vibration of any state at will. This is a powerful tool. The Law of Polarity is also why it is so important to be strong in your vibration and vibrate at the highest level possible. Think of the temperature example. If you are really hot, it will take a lot of cold to cool you off.

SOUL SOOTHER

Your soul is working hard to help you evolve. A large part of evolution depends on your vibratory rate. When you understand how the Law of Polarity works, you can see how other people's vibrations can move you up or down your own vibratory pole. By taking charge of your vibration, you can be a positive influence on your environment. The importance of being in control of your vibration, especially as far as your life purpose, cannot be understated. You can be a positive conscious force, creating harmony and offering light as you move through your day, or you can be a mindless tornado, wreaking havoc. Your soul is happiest when you are able to use your vibration in a conscious way to shine your light and be a leading, positive influence on everyone and thing you encounter! What a wonderful loving gift you can be for your environment.

One way to ensure that you are vibrating at the highest level is to use the Chakra Meditations found in the next chapter.

CHAPTER 17

The Chakra Meditations

The mysteries of resonance and time vibrate our essence. Past and future teachers work with higher frequencies and when we experience them they burn in our hearts. When we achieve more lift in our vibration our heart rings with love like the striking of a bell.

— *DAVID BENNETT, Voyage of Purpose*

The Chakra Meditation – Healing Color

1. Inhale deeply and with each exhalation feel your shoulders relaxing.
2. Return to breathing normally.
3. Inhale and imagine that you are breathing in healing green light.
4. Allow the green light to go into your body on a cellular level, swirling around like scrubbing bubbles.
5. Continue to breathe in and out as you visualize the green light expanding throughout your body.
6. Once your body is full of healing green light, on your next out-breath, imagine all the *dis*-ease, discordant energy, tension, and frustration leave your body and be sent to the light to be transmuted into healing energy for you.
7. Repeat for a total of three cycles of healing green light.
8. Repeat the process again with golden light for another three cycles to act as a soothing and loving finish.
9. Remember to ask the Recycling Angels to come and clean up!

The Chakra Meditation – Balancing the Chakras

Due to the length of this meditation, it might be better read into a recorder and played back when you want to use it.

1. Inhale deeply and with each exhalation feel your shoulders relaxing.
2. Return to breathing normally.
3. Imagine a vibrant rainbow above your head with all the colors: red, orange, yellow, green, light blue, indigo, and violet.
4. See the red of the rainbow enter the top of your head, known as your Crown Chakra. Allow it to fill your body from head to toe, like scrubbing bubbles.
5. Focusing on the base of your spine, allow the red light to clear and clean the Root Chakra with the intention that you have all the energy you need for your tasks today.
6. Exhale and release the blockages and lower vibrational energy that has been cleared or cleansed.
7. Repeat the process, bringing in orange light, focus on your pelvic area and intend a strong ability to positively connect with those you meet today.
8. Exhale, releasing anything that has been cleared or cleansed.
9. Bring in Yellow, focused on your stomach. This time ask that you use your power well, knowing when to stand up for yourself and when to let things go.
10. Release anything that has been cleared or cleansed, as you exhale.
11. Focus on your heart and visualizing the light coming from the rainbow, as you choose a green color that feels soothing to you.

12. Intend that you are able to see the interconnectedness of all you meet and bring the most loving energy you can to any situation you are in.
13. Exhale and release anything that has been cleared or cleansed.
14. Feel your throat muscles relaxing as the blue light enters the top of your head and fills your entire body. Ask that you have the ability to express your truth in a way that is compassionate and clear.
15. Exhale, releasing anything that has been cleared or cleansed.
16. Bring in the indigo light. It will fill you entirely yet spend more time around your head than the rest of your body.
17. Focusing just above your eyes, ask that you be open to all the guidance available to you from your soul, guides, and angels.
18. Release anything that has been cleared or cleansed, as you exhale.
19. Ask that you be guided by your highest potential, as the violet light enters and pervades your body, especially at the top of your head.
20. Exhale, releasing anything that has been cleared or cleansed.
21. Finish by taking a moment to ground yourself with either your roots or red cord.

WHERE AND WHEN

The Chakra Meditations can be thought of as maintenance for the body's Energetic System. Similar to getting an oil change every 3,000 miles, you benefit from doing some sort of Chakra Meditation regularly. Just as you wash your car when it is dirty, you can use a Chakra Meditation to clean up whenever you are not feeling your best. Besides basic maintenance, the Chakra Meditations are helpful to boost your energy when someone around you has a cold or you are not feeling well. The Chakra Meditations can be especially helpful in that crucial time when you feel that first throat tickle. Yet no meditation is a substitute for going to the doctor. Think of the Chakra Meditations as your energy cleaners and boosters. If you have been around someone who is pushy or needy, either Chakra Meditation will help minimize the effect of that person.

You can practice your Chakra Meditations whenever you do not need your attention to be focused outwardly. You can use other colors in the Chakra Healing Color Meditation depending on the issue you are working on, but green, white, and gold work the best. *Do not use platinum or diamond colors unless familiar with the side effects.* Neither meditation is to be used while driving, as your focus will be inward and not paying attention to your surroundings. If you want to get the most of your Chakra Meditations, focus your intent to manifest healing by using the color associated with the Chakra corresponding to the issue you are working on. In the example of the Healing Color Meditation, green is used. Green relates to the Heart Chakra and helps you feel love and compassion toward yourself and others. When you set your intention for love and compassion along with using the color green as you inhale and exhale, it will strengthen the effect of the meditation.

EXAMPLE

Jessica has been feeling low on energy for a few days now. Going to school for her Master's and working full-time is taking its toll. To top it off, it seems that everyone on the bus is sniffling and sneezing. She knows she can't get sick right now; work is crazy and she has a paper due before the break. Jessica promises herself she will get to bed before midnight and since she still has quite a few bus stops before the campus, decides to do the Chakra Balancing

Meditation. Picturing a rainbow over her head, she starts by pulling the vibrant red color from the rainbow into her lungs as she breathes in red. Jessica likes using the breath to bring in the color instead of through the top of the head. Allowing the red color to permeate every cell in her body, she sees them as red scrubbing bubbles. She exhales all that is cleaned and asks the recycling angels to clean up. Next she pulls in the pumpkin orange from the rainbow, repeating the process with sunny yellow, grassy green, sky blue, indigo blue, and violet. She ends with a beautiful golden light that she imagines coming from a golden Buddha sitting above the rainbow. She still has two stops; so she allows the golden light to fill her up, surrounding her for a minute before it dissipates. She calls in the recycling angels one more time, for a final cleanup while reminding herself of her promise to go to bed tonight before the clock strikes midnight!

WHY – CHAKRAS WITHIN THE PHYSICAL BODY

You can think of Chakras as facilitators for energy to come into and leave your body. There are seven main Chakras in the physical body, along with hundreds of other Chakras in your physical and non-physical bodies. The first three Chakras in the non-physical body will be discussed in the next chapter.

If you could imagine someone dropping a plumb line from the top of your head and down through your body, it would come out between your legs. That line is the Sushumna, which is the highway used by the energy brought in by the Chakras to travel through the body. Like any highway, there are roads that branch off from exits. Think of the exits as the Chakras and the highways and minor roads as the major and minor Nadis. For this discussion, we are going to focus on the main highway and the exits—or the Sushumna and the Chakras.

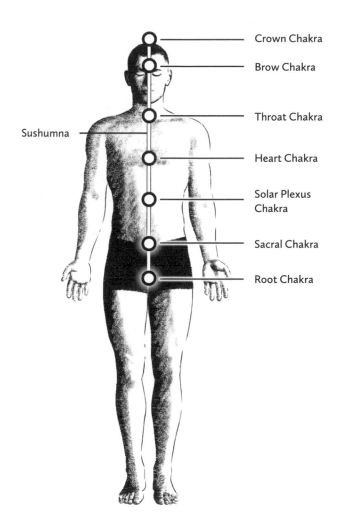

Crown Chakra

Brow Chakra

Throat Chakra

Sushumna

Heart Chakra

Solar Plexus
Chakra

Sacral Chakra

Root Chakra

Each Chakra is assigned to transport energy to and from different organs and parts of the body. Chakras can be visualized as vortexes, although they are energetic. Chakras won't be found on an x-ray or CAT scan, yet can be seen by those who are sensitive to Chakra

energy or the aura. Most often these people are healers or intu-
itives. Yet sometimes I come across a person who has seen auras
since birth. He or she sees a person's Chakra energy most often in
the form of colors.

There are no absolutes with chakras, yet some basic concepts
about the seven main Chakras in the physical body are accepted
by most systems. Not all cultures agree on the specific details, so if
you follow a different tradition, that is okay. When working with
Chakras in meditation, it is best to use the colors, names, and loca-
tions you are most comfortable with, no matter what any book says.

Chakras have their own vibratory rates, rising faster and higher
as you move up the Sushumna. Of the seven main Chakras in the
body, the Chakra with the slowest rate is the Root Chakra and the
fastest vibratory rate is the Crown Chakra. These two have only
one direction. The Root Chakra points downward and mostly deals
with Earth Energy. The Crown Chakra points upward and deals
with Spirit or Universal Energy. The other five Chakras have a
front and back. The rear of the Chakra is usually a little smaller
than the front entrance, and sometimes the back of the Chakra is
located slightly lower on the back of your body.

Each Chakra deals with a different type of consciousness, organ,
color, food, tone, etc. The idea is that these elements should be balanced, so even though you want to strengthen your solar plexus using
the food of the solar plexus Chakra, starch, and the color, yellow, it
doesn't give you a free pass to binge on cookies or wear bright yellow every day! You need to balance your starch intake and using a
vibrant yellow in your Chakra Healing Color Meditation will help
invigorate the solar plexus, where a soft yellow will calm it down.

The easiest way to work with a chakra is to use the associated
color in the Chakra Healing Color Meditation, while balancing its
corresponding food in your diet. You can also wear the color, or a

crystal with that same color, and vocalize using the corresponding tone. Bringing the element of the Chakra into your life also works. If you are working with the Root Chakra, the related element is Earth. Go play in the garden for a bit! If you start working with the healthy attributes of the Chakra by emulating them in daily life, that will also help empower that Chakra. You can make yourself a Chakra prescription of sorts, by using the information below, or referring to the Chakra chart on the next page. Working with a Chakra is never a substitute for traditional medical care, yet Chakra healing can support whatever mainstream treatments you are using.

Trouble with a particular Chakra can show up through disease or malfunction in the body parts or organs related to the particular Chakra. It is important to remember that a Chakra cannot be totally blocked or totally open without major illness. I have people tell me that a psychic told them their Chakra is blocked, or their aura is dark, and for X amount of dollars the "psychic" will fix it. This ridiculousness is what gives psychics a bad name. If a Chakra was totally blocked you would be dead, or in the hospital at best, and everyone has a bad day with a gloomy aura. The best thing you can do to avoid a clogged-up Chakra or dull aura is to do your Chakra Meditations, eat well, get enough rest, laugh, love, and live your life as fully as possible. There is something called a Kundalini Awakening that can leave your Chakras blown open if you are not prepared for it, yet this is rare and can create a mental imbalance if not activated properly. The Chakra Meditations in this book are meant to be gentle, safe, and loving. As with any meditation, never push. Let the meditation be natural, slow, and smooth. One does not approach meditation like a 50-yard dash. It is important to remember that no one is totally blocked or totally healthy in any Chakra. It is a constant balancing act, so you might see a little of yourself in all of these Chakra traits, both weak and strong.

The Seven Main Chakras

Chakra	Color	Food	Element	Tone	Outer Body	Organ	Body Parts	Consciousness
Root	Red	Protein	Earth	O - oh	Etheric	Adrenal	Bones, Large intestine, Fleshy parts	Security, Groundedness, Vitality
Sacral	Orange	Water	Water	Oo - due	Emotional	Reproductive	Body Fluids, Circulation, Genitals	Emotions, Sexuality, Sociability
Solar Plexus	Yellow	Starch	Fire	Ah - father	Lower Mental	Adrenal	Metabolic and Digestive System	Mental Control, Personal Power, Will
Heart	Green	Vegetables	Air	Aye - play	Higher Mental	Thymus	Heart, Lungs, Chest, Breathing	Love & Compassion
Throat	Sky Blue	Fruit	Ether & Sound	Ee - we	Lower Intuitive	Thyroid	Throat, Ears, Taste, Neck & Shoulders	Communication, Truth, Creativity, Clairaudience
Brow	Indigo	Meditation	Light	Mmm - hem	Higher Intuitive	Pineal	Eyes, Forehead, Sinus	Clairvoyance & Imagination
Crown	Violet	Fasting	Knowing	Nngh - sing	Transcendent	Pituitary	Top of head	Connection to Spirit

What follows is a descriptive account of the seven main Chakras within the physical body. Starting with the first Chakra closest to the ground and with the slowest vibration, the **ROOT CHAKRA,** also known as *Muladhara*, meaning root or support, is located at the base of the spine. In the system I am using, the color is red, the food is protein, and the element is earth. If you want a tone to support the Root Chakra, you would use "O" as in Oh. Remember that different traditions have different colors, tones, etc. Use what works best for you. In the remaining chapters you will learn about the Outer Bodies, which are bodies outside the physical body, and the Root Chakra is connected to the Etheric Body, the first, and closest, of the outer bodies. The consciousness of this Chakra is security, groundedness, and vitality. It is here that you develop your roots and the feeling that you belong here. You develop your sense of "being." The main gland associated with the Root Chakra is the adrenal, a responsibility shared with the solar plexus. The body parts it is responsible for are the bones, large intestines, and fleshy parts. Just for fun, people have noticed that the seven Chakras correspond with the energies of the Seven Dwarfs in Disney's *Snow White*. The Root Chakra is Grumpy. We connect with the Root Chakra when we are worried about security, don't feel well, or anything having to deal with the physical body's energy level. If your Root Chakra is strong, you usually have no trouble supporting yourself, have a good self-image, and trust in others without being naive. If your Root Chakra is weak, you might have issues with security, difficulty trusting, out of proportional need for material things, and a touch of self-centeredness.

THE SACRAL CHAKRA, or *Svadhisthana,* meaning sweetness, has a slightly higher vibration, and is located between the pelvic bone and the belly button. In my system, the color is orange, the food is water, and so is the element. The tone is "oo" as in due. The consciousness is emotion, sexuality, sociability, and reproduction. The Sacral Chakra corresponds to the Emotional Body. It is here that you develop an understanding of "Other." This Chakra activates when, as an infant, you first start to relate to other people. This is where you develop your position in the family, your outer identity, as well as how to express emotion. The Sacral Chakra is in charge of the reproductive organs, as well as bodily fluids, circulation, urination, genitals, and fertility. We often engage the Sacral Chakra when we are relating to others or dealing with our own sexuality. The Dwarf for this Chakra is Bashful! A weak Sacral Chakra can create uncertainty about your sexuality, a difficulty in expressing your needs, and trouble expressing emotions. A strong Sacral Chakra allows you to have a healthy attitude toward sex, a happy and kind personality, with a strong connection to your emotions.

THE SOLAR PLEXUS, or *Manipura*, meaning lustrous gem, is our personal power Chakra. It lies between your belly button and rib cage and becomes active at two to three years of age. The color is sunny yellow, the food is starch, and the element is fire. The tone is "ah" as in father. The Lower Mental Body is the Outer Body association, while the physical associations of this Chakra are the adrenal glands, metabolic system, digestive system, and stomach. The Dwarf for this Chakra is Sneezy, known for the powerful force behind his sneeze. The consciousness is mental control, personal power, and use of will. You will often deal with this Chakra when you feel threatened. It is your place of flight or fight. This is where you get butterflies when you have to exert your will in a difficult situation and why your tummy gets upset when you feel nervous. When this Chakra is not thriving, you could develop difficulty trusting the natural flow of life, tend to dominate others or cower, and need to be in control of life situations or give your power over to others. When the Solar Plexus is working well, you are tolerant of others while knowing when to stand up for yourself, when to back off, when to allow others to be in control, and you have a strong sense of your true value.

THE HEART CHAKRA, or *Anahata*, meaning unstruck, is located, you guessed it, in the middle of your chest. You may have noticed that when you are in a heartbreaking situation, the pain is in the middle of the chest, not over your actual heart. It is your Heart Chakra that reacts to situations where your compassion kicks in and is activated around four to five years old. The color is green, the food is vegetables, and the element is air. These associations are called upon when someone has a heart attack. Doctors often recommend eating more vegetables and getting out for some fresh air. The tone is "aye" as in play. The Outer Body is the Higher Mental Body. The consciousness of this Chakra is love (different than lust) and compassion. This is the type of love that a person feels for humanity or a tree; it is a universal love. The parts of the body related to the Heart Chakra are the heart, heartbeat, lungs, chest, breath, and the gland is the thymus. You activate this Chakra with feelings of unconditional love. When the Heart Chakra is not in harmony, you might have trouble accepting love from others and giving love without conditions. The healthy Heart Chakra typically does not look for rewards when doing loving things, is able to accept love, help, and assistance without the fear of owing anything, and maintains a strong balance between material and spiritual worlds. Happy is the Dwarf associated with the Heart Chakra.

THE THROAT CHAKRA, located in the area of the throat, is also known as *Visuddha*, meaning purification. This Chakra's color is sky blue, also known as cerulean blue. The food is fruit; the element is ether and sound, with the tone being "eee" as in we. For ether, think of the space between the molecules, not what mothers used to be given for pain during childbirth. The consciousness is about communicating your truth, creativity, clairaudience, and

Divine Will. It is activated when one learns to speak truths, usually the teen years. The main communicator of the Seven Dwarfs was Doc, and he is the dwarf for the Throat Chakra. The Throat Chakra supplies energy to the throat, ears, taste buds, neck, and shoulders, while influencing the thyroid gland. Many children who are not able to speak up develop Thyroid problems. A friend of mine lived in a house where, like many of us, children were to be seen but not heard. She had thyroid problems all her life. By starting to speak her truth, working with cerulean blue light in her Chakra Healing Meditation, and with her doctor's approval, she was able to reduce her thyroid medication as she began to heal her thyroid condition. If you are having trouble with your Throat Chakra, you might find that no matter how much you talk, you can't get your thoughts across. Also, you might not communicate your truth even when asked. Silence may make you uncomfortable or visa versa. Being this is the purification Chakra, often the Throat Chakra comes into play when dealing with addictions or when working on allowing "Thy Will, not my will." If your Throat Chakra is strong, you know how to balance silence with talking, are good at self-expression, and do not fear speaking your truth. A thriving Throat Chakra coincides with strong creativity and ability to communicate your intuition.

THE BROW CHAKRA, commonly called the Third Eye, is also known as *Ajna*, meaning to perceive. As the name implies, this is where a lot of your intuition enters the body. It is located above the eyebrows in the center of the forehead and its color is indigo, although sometimes purple is used. The food is meditation, the element is light, and the tone is "mmm." This Chakra, along with the Crown Chakra is not necessarily activated at a specific age. The gland is the Pineal Gland, which affects the melatonin level in our system, and so the Dwarf is Sleepy. The consciousness of this Chakra relates to intuition, clairvoyance, and imagination. It is in charge of the eyes, forehead, and sinus. Sometimes you can get headaches, especially above the eyebrows, when trying too hard to access your Third Eye, yet not every migraine is a Brow Chakra issue. An unhealthy Brow Chakra can lead to not connecting with your inner wisdom, rejection of spiritual ideas, and depending only on what you see with your physical eyes. A healthy Brow Chakra usually has no trouble trusting intuition, the ability to see with more than their physical eyes, and a strong connection with their spiritual side, guides, and inner wisdom.

THE CROWN CHAKRA is at the top of the head, where your soft spot was as a child. Also called *Sahasrara*, meaning thousand-fold, this Chakra is seen as violet or white. Sometimes gold will even be seen. In the next chapter, you will learn why gold is closely associated with the Crown Chakra. This is the fastest vibrating Chakra in the physical body and consciousness is of the highest level, being your connection to Spirit and higher knowledge. Fasting is the "food" and the element is "knowing." Toning uses the sound "nngh" as in sing. The gland is the pituitary or master gland. You access your Crown Chakra to bring the highest universal energies into the body and during channeling of angels and other spirit guides. It is unusual that this Chakra is extremely unhealthy or extraordinarily healthy, although a sickly Crown Chakra could result in extreme depression, anxiety, and an inability to feel comforted by the knowledge of a higher power. A superhuman type of Crown Chakra would allow for a strong connection to your higher self and all that Spirit can offer. You would have a strong ability to experience cosmic consciousness and interconnectedness instead of intellectually understanding it. Most of us have an average Crown Chakra that works on autopilot until we focus on training it.

SOUL SOOTHER

Working with the Chakras, making sure they are balanced and healthy, is one of the best things you can do for your spiritual growth. With a clear Energetic System, you vibrate at a higher level and your guides can work with you, both physically and energetically, with greater ease. Your guides are vibrating at a very high level; for example, if you can imagine a seven-foot man trying to give a hug to a two-year-old sitting on the floor, that is comparable to your guides trying to give you support. They need to lower their vibrations down to your level. It is easier for them to connect with you when you are vibrating at a higher level, just as it is easier for the man to give a hug when the child stands up on a chair. With your Chakras clear, you can process lower vibrations with greater ease, thereby avoiding being dragged down by people and situations that are not for your highest and most loving good. All of this allows your soul to focus on your chosen life path while raising your vibration and receiving the most help from your guides as possible.

There are Chakras above the physical body, and the Golden Light Meditation will access them, helping bring a loving and protective energy around you while raising your vibration even higher.

CHAPTER 18

The Golden Light Meditation

*Do we feel the connection and love of the divine energy
from the universe? It's a steadfast call from our soul
singing to us through our hearts to melt the insecurity
and weakness. It buoys us up in times of challenge and
stress. It feeds our awakening souls and encourages us
to continue moving on our paths. Let us take a moment
each day.. each hour.. to connect and fill our cups so we
may be fully present.*

— DAVID BENNETT, *Voyage of Purpose*

The Golden Light Meditation

1. Take three deep breaths, and with each exhale, feel your shoulders relax.
2. Return to breathing normally.
3. Imagine a source of golden light above you. It can be a star, a pitcher of light, or even an angel's hand.
4. Know that golden light holds the protective energy of Unconditional Love.
5. Place your awareness on the top of your head.
6. Imagine that the loving and protective golden light is flowing down from above and entering into the top of your head.
7. Visualize your entire head filling up with the golden light.
8. Imagine your body is like a balloon, empty and ready to be filled.

9. Let the golden light continue to flow from above, through your neck and then into your chest. The loving golden light is filling you up like a beautiful golden balloon.

10. Allow the golden light to continue, filling your belly, hips, and bottom, traveling down through your legs, and filling up your toes.

11. Allow the golden light to continue to come in the top of your head. When you feel that you are so filled with golden light that you are about to burst, let it flow out through your pores and your physical body.

12. Let the loving golden light flow out of your physical body and imagine it forming a circle of protective and loving light around you.

13. Ensure that the golden light fills your circle equally above, behind, in front of, and below you.

14. Focus on the light entering with each inhale and expand your circle of light during the exhale, if it is easier.

15. Imagine your circle of golden light is as full, bright, and loving as it can be.

16. Intend the flow of golden light to stop flowing into the top of your head.

17. Allow yourself the luxury of simply sitting in the golden energy of Unconditional Love for as long as you wish.

18. Imagine the golden light dissipating.

19. Ask the Recycling Angels to clear up anything that is cleared and cleansed during this meditation. Or, you can ask that all that is cleansed and cleared be sent back to the light and returned as healing energies.

WHERE AND WHEN

Have you ever felt drained after a lunch with Negative Nellie or a meeting with Bossy Brad? This is the time for the Golden Light Meditation. The Golden Light Meditation will help refill your cup after an undesirable or unhealthy situation. It is also a wonderful meditation when you are working on increasing your intuition or self-value. The whole meditation can be done in just a minute or two after you get used to it or, if you enjoy it, you can prolong it as long as you like. I like to start my day with the Golden Light Meditation, and the shower is the perfect place. You have to shower anyway, so you might as well fill your cup with Unconditional Love! Simply imagine the water flowing from the showerhead is golden light and the drain acts like the Recycling Angel. It is easiest to do this meditation with your eyes closed, although if you are not alone, try it with your eyes open. Waiting in line, after lunch, when you have been around draining people, or before you go into the house are prime times to do this meditation. I recommend using the Golden Light Meditation a number of times throughout your day. You can't overdose from Golden Light!

EXAMPLE

Pam promises her Aunt Lillian that she will take her to the doctor today, even though she still has to pick up the kids and make dinner. She knows her aunt doesn't ask for help unless it is really needed, yet, while waiting for Aunt Lillian at the doctor's office, Pam starts resenting her for intruding on her busy day. Pam looks around the waiting room, observes that everyone looks a little cranky - the lady in the corner has a definite scowl. The more Pam thinks about it, the more she ruminates on how no one ever tries to make her day easier. Pam sees a tacky gold-colored lamp by the magazines and remembers the Golden Light Meditation. She decides to do something for herself for a change and imagines golden light flowing from a beautiful crystal chandelier above her head and down through her body. She fills herself with Unconditional Love until she thinks she will burst. Then she expands the golden light out of her body and lets it fill the entire waiting room. She asks that everything not for her highest and most loving good be cleared and cleansed. Pam remembers that although she thinks loving energy feels nice, if a person isn't used to being loved, it can feel uncomfortable. So she adds a caveat: "in a way that will not be felt as intrusive to anyone else in the room." She also asks that the golden light be for the highest good for all those coming into the waiting room. She feels her heart opening wide from all the loving energy of the golden light. She knows, deep inside, she has enough time to do all that is required from her today and she is happy to help out her favorite aunt. She feels a little silly imagining the Recycling Angels swooping around the doctor's office, picking up the cleared energy, so she intends that all cleansed and cleared be sent to the light to come back as healing energy for those in the waiting room. When she has finished her meditation and looks around again, people seem more relaxed, the woman with the scowl in the corner has drifted off to sleep, and that tacky lamp doesn't look quite so bad!

WHY – CHAKRAS OUTSIDE THE PHYSICAL BODY

Why is golden light so important? In the previous chapter on Chakras, you learned of the seven main Chakras within the physical body. There are seven Chakras above the body as well. The first three will be dealt with here, including the Golden Chakra, the Platinum Chakra, and the Diamond Chakra. Like the Chakras within the body, spiritual systems describe the Chakras outside the physical body differently. Use the information that feels right to you.

It might be easier if you could imagine the Chakras outside of the body as the magnet for the energy to condense around and then disperse from, rather than as a vortex to bring the energy through. When you call on the energy of these upper Chakras, they spread their vibration and energy through the whole body, more like the ripple of a pond than rain on an umbrella. Think of it as a pattern within your existing energy field. It shifts your existing energy rather than adds to it. Because these Chakras are not within the physical body, they react to each person differently. This creates a problem when you are trying to describe them. Bear that in mind as you continue to read.

THE GOLDEN CHAKRA is the first Chakra above the Crown Chakra and the vibration is considerably faster and higher. Golden light is often found in the Crown Chakra because of this closeness. The Golden Chakra is the Chakra of Spirit's unconditional love for you and assists you to pass that unconditional love on to others. You don't need to follow a particular faith to imagine that there is a great loving energy available to us all. The Golden Chakra is your direct connection to that loving energy. The golden light from this Chakra can be warming and feels exceptionally loving and safe. You can actually use the Golden Light Meditation when you are cold. Using golden light from the Golden Chakra can also help you to purify your intent. You might be tempted to send energy of a particular color to someone, but you may not know what is best for him or her. Asking that golden light be sent to someone is safer. Golden light is Unconditional Love, so it is helpful for bringing a person back into balance and into a place of feeling loved. Yet, it is always best to ask the person's guide to send the golden light instead of you sending it. If you want to know how this is done, see the diagram in the chapter for the Staying in Your Energy Meditation. Golden light is protective and a common choice for setting up an aura of protection around you when doing spiritual work. You cannot overdose on golden light, which is one reason why the Golden Light Meditation is the first Light Meditation given to those who want to learn how to channel.

THE PLATINUM CHAKRA is the next higher vibration above the Golden Chakra. This Chakra relates to Spiritual Courage or courage of the heart. Not the bungee-jumping, risk-taking type of courage. It is the courage to tell your family about your real spiritual beliefs, your sexual preference, or that you are not going into the family business. It is the courage to speak your truth about what lies deepest in your heart, even when you know others may not want to know. It is the courage to allow your divine spark to be the light that illuminates your path.

Some have trouble visualizing platinum. Think of silver, yet without the gray tone. Or go to a jeweler and ask to see a platinum ring. Platinum light does not have a temperature or feeling like the golden light. Light from the Platinum Chakra is best called upon when courage to speak your truth is needed. You may also use platinum light when you want to work with the higher energies, guides, and masters. Platinum light is a type of engager to activate your soul's light. It is a clearing energy that, unlike golden light, you can overdo and create a healing crisis. I recommend that you do not work with platinum light unless you have a teacher to work along with you.

So, unlike golden light, you can overdose on platinum light. When working with platinum light, you may not feel it, yet the results will show up within a week or two. I teach how to use the platinum light in my spiritual and psychic development classes, always warning students that if they have uncontrollable urges to tell off their mother-in-laws, they need to cut back on the platinum light. Courage is great, but so is diplomacy.

THE DIAMOND CHAKRA is the highest and fastest vibration of the three discussed here. It represents the unbreakable bond between you and your creator. You cannot change who you are born from. Even if you don't know who your mother is, your mother has died, or you choose to ignore her, someone birthed you. This is also true of whatever you call a Divine Creator. You can refuse to believe in a Creator, you can ignore a Creator, yet you cannot become uncreated. Nothing you do, don't do, or someone else does, can interfere with that bond. Even in death, you have been created. Diamond light represents that unbreakable bond. As for the color of the Diamond Chakra, if you can imagine how a diamond sparkles and add that sparkle to a clear bright light containing sparkles of every color imaginable, you would have diamond light.

You can feel diamond light. It may feel warm, but it will not physically warm you like golden light. It feels more like the clear, clean air after a storm, similar to how it would feel to have no toxins in your body, or what drinking absolutely clean water tastes like. Diamond light is a transmuting force. It will transmute your lower vibrations to a higher level. It can help clear you of anxiety, raise your vibration when you want to learn to channel, and manifest the situations needed to clear karma. As a diamond is able to cut through almost anything, diamond light works like Drano for the soul and should be used cautiously and very sparingly. It corresponds with the personal will of the Solar Plexus Chakra, and we can be forceful with what we want, so it is necessary to be cautious when using diamond light. Also, because of its connection to your metabolism, if you use it before you are ready, or in too great a concentration, it can create a strong flu-like symptom or other healing crisis. When you need to break through an issue that has been blocking you, you can use diamond light. Remember, use it sparingly and better yet, just a tiny bit mixed with golden light. If you are like many, you want to break through your issues now, to get it over with all at once. Yet remember that Spirit will give you what you ask for, so I recommend that you be patient with your growth. Work on yourself slowly and consistently, allowing your evolution to flow naturally, without forcing it. As suggested, mix diamond light with golden light and ask that it assist you in a way that is gentle and loving for all those concerned.

The golden light is not less or more than diamond or platinum light. Each Chakra above the body and its corresponding light has a different purpose. They are also not less or more than the seven main Chakras, yet using them wisely and responsibly, combining the colors of the Chakras outside the physical body with either the Golden Light Meditation or the upcoming Light Work Meditations, can help you raise your vibration in ways that are not accessible with the rainbow colors of the physical body's Chakras.

You have already learned ways to use the Chakras and specifically their colors. When using the Golden Light Meditation, you can substitute the different Chakras' colors depending on what you want to achieve. I strongly recommend that you choose wisely and avoid using the platinum and diamond light until you have mastered the Chakras within the body and the Golden Chakra. Even then, use the platinum and diamond lights sparingly.

SOUL SOOTHER

Learning how to use the Chakras above the body allows a level of clearing that can open you to deep communication with your soul. This communication may be through your guides, your intuition, or your angels. As discussed in the section on intuition, it may come through hearing, sensing, seeing, or knowing. Adding the higher Chakra vibrations into your meditations allows you to attain higher levels of vibration and clearer communication with your divine guidance. When you can receive your soul and guides' communication with greater clarity, it is easier to recognize the signs they leave, assisting you to make the choices that offer the highest and most loving opportunities for you to fulfill your soul's plan.

Once you have cleared the Chakras within and above the body, addressing your Outer Bodies with the meditation in the next chapter will complete the clearing of your entire Energetic System.

CHAPTER 19

The Outer Bodies Meditation

We forget our essence. Our true being is beyond
form, beyond the content that exists with form and
beyond time. Our true being is limitless.
When we develop the practice of daily connection
to our being, we are on the path of conscious
awakening and exploring our expansion.
— *DAVID BENNETT*, Voyage of Purpose

The Outer Bodies Meditation

1. Take three deep breaths, and with each exhalation, relax your shoulders.
2. Return to breathing normally.
3. Close your eyes. Intend that the space you are in be surrounded with beautiful and protective golden light.
4. Imagine yourself floating comfortably inside a bubble. You can see through the walls, as they are translucent and slightly opalescent. There is also a wand floating nearby.
5. Create equal space between you and the side of the bubble below you, above you, and side-to-side. Check that the space is uniform behind and in front of you.
6. Bring a guide or helper with you, if you want, by just imagining them there. If anyone or thing is in your bubble that you do not want, tell it to be gone and it will leave. This is your sacred space.

7. Start to look around. If your bubble feels confined, exhale fully and the walls of your bubble will expand. Again ensure that there is equal room all around you.
8. Point the wand you find next to you at anything you do not want in your bubble and it will disappear.
9. Use your breath if your bubble needs more light; as you exhale imagine the bubble fill with more light.
10. Look at the quality and texture of the walls of your bubble. Is there anything that doesn't look right to you?
11. Pass your hand over the irregularity; you will generate a beautiful, opalescent, fluidic light that fixes anything that doesn't seem right.
12. Take another look around and if there is anything you think is off, allow yourself a moment to fix it.
13. Take a few moments to simply be calm, comfortable, and aware of your space.
14. Before you move around too much, do a quick Grounding Meditation.
15. Open your eyes when you are ready.

WHERE AND WHEN

You don't need to be at home to use the Outer Bodies Meditation, yet you want to be in a space where you feel safe and will not be disturbed. You could try the car, a restroom, or a quiet park. I like to do the Outer Bodies Meditation first thing in the morning or at the end of the day, but I also use it if I find myself feeling drained. Sometimes you can feel like the world is against you, and that is the optimum time to go inward and work on cleaning up your bubble. If you feel you have been around negativity or other unwanted energies, take the time to do the Outer Bodies Meditation. This, along with the Chakra Meditations, is a type of

Light Work meditation (more will be taught about Light Work in the next chapter). Whether you are working on your physical self or energetic Outer Bodies, Light Work–style meditations are real and will have tangible affects. You may find that the Outer Bodies Meditation works best when you know you have as much time as you need to do the clearing. Although if you do this meditation regularly you will find that you can accomplish it in just a minute or two.

EXAMPLE

Thomas goes to a "peace" meeting with a friend, and to his surprise, it ends up being a group of very angry people. Thomas, feeling that it doesn't help to have a fight-club mentality when you are trying to promote peace, speaks his truth in a compassionate way. Yet a number of people are angry at him. When he gets home, he does his nightly Review Meditation and decides he could not have done a better job speaking his truth, so he tries to let the whole thing go. Yet Thomas's mind keeps being drawn back into the drama of the night. He feels as if he can't get away from the anger that some of the group expressed. Thomas decides to do the Outer Bodies Meditation to make sure that the anger of the group is not in his Energetic System. When he goes into his bubble, he notices that it isn't as clear and opalescent as usual. He takes a moment to breathe light and space into his bubble and decides to do the Golden Light Meditation while still inside his bubble. When he finishes, he looks around for anything else that might be unusual, yet the Golden Light Meditation seems to have returned his bubble to the right translucence, size, and brightness. Thomas comes out of the meditation and also does the Blessing Meditation for his apartment just for good measure. Everything feels much better as he is finally able to let go of tonight's drama and falls quickly to sleep.

WHY – THE OUTER BODIES

Your Energetic System contains more than highways and exits, Sushumna and Chakras — it also has the Outer Bodies. Think of these as restaurants, each catering to a different taste. Just like you can find a good Italian restaurant in almost any neighborhood, the Outer Bodies are not located in one specific location. Yet, if you really want good Italian food, you might take the "Little Italy" exit off the highway. Each Chakra is connected to a specific Outer Body, similar to an exit being associated with a specific neighborhood. Each of your Outer Bodies is also connected to you physically, emotionally, mentally, intuitively, and spiritually.

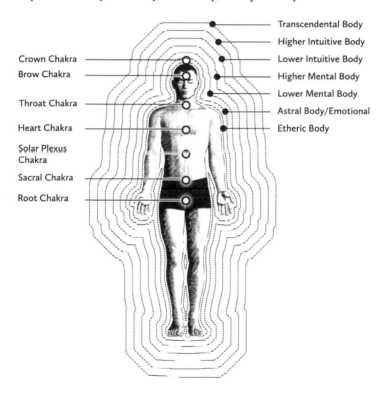

Crown Chakra

Brow Chakra

Throat Chakra

Heart Chakra

Solar Plexus Chakra

Sacral Chakra

Root Chakra

Transcendental Body

Higher Intuitive Body

Lower Intuitive Body

Higher Mental Body

Lower Mental Body

Astral Body/Emotional

Etheric Body

Understanding the Chakra–Outer Body association will allow you to work on strengthening a particular Outer Body by bolstering the associated Chakra and vice versa. In order to visualize the Outer Bodies, many people picture them as a seven-layer cake. They are, however, more like the Chakras outside the physical body: their energy permeates your entire body.

The basic supply of energy for the physical body comes in through the Transcendent Outer Body, moving through the Intuitive Bodies, the Mental Bodies, the Emotional Body and finally into your physical body through the Etheric Body. With that said, the energy level of each Chakra is also affected by the energy level of its associated Outer Body. If the outer body is weak, you will find that the energy of the associated Chakra will most likely be weak.

You also receive guidance, passed down through the Outer Bodies. Think of your guides whispering instructions into your Transcendent Body like in the game of Telephone. Each Outer Body passes along the message, slightly colored by their perception, down to the Outer Body below it. The information finally arrives through the Etheric Body and if the outer bodies are not strong and clear, the message can be distorted.

Physical	Chakra	Outer Body	Strength
Gland & Hormone Regulation	Crown	Transcendent	Above understanding
Eyes & Sinus	Brow	Higher Intuitive	Direct Messages from Guides, Master, and Angels
Neck, Ears & Throat	Throat	Lower Intuitive	Intuition, Gut feelings, Psychic information
Heart, Lung, & Blood Pressure	Heart	Higher Mental	Spiritual & Societal beliefs
Metabolism, Digestion, & Stomach	Solar Plexus	Lower Mental	Everyday thoughts, fears, and beliefs
Fertility, Circulation, & Fluids	Sacral	Emotional	Emotions
Bones, Flesh, & Vitality	Root	Etheric	Energy level

Similar to how energy from the Outer Body strengthens the corresponding Chakra, certain information or strengths are offered to you through each of the Outer Bodies.

For example, intuition having to do with daily life is accessed via the Throat Chakra and the Lower Intuitive Body. Similarly, the Higher Mental Body provides access to your beliefs about society and spirituality through the Heart Chakra. There is an integral connection between Chakras and Outer Bodies.

Also, if you are overthinking, which is associated with the Lower Mental Body, you may find a drain on the Emotional and Etheric bodies as the Lower Mental Body is using more energy and so less energy is passed along to the bodies below it.

The rate of vibration rises as you go out further into the Outer Bodies. The Etheric Body will be the slowest vibratory rate, one of the reasons it is easiest to see, with the Transcendent Body vibrating at such a fast rate that it is, for the most part, inaccessible. The faster the vibration, like a pinwheel spinning more and more quickly, the more it is perceived as just a blur. The Transcendent Body is vibrating so fast, it cannot be observed.

If you need healing in one Outer Body, the answer is to look to the strength of the Outer Body "above" it. If you are struggling with your emotions, which in turn weaken the Emotional Body, then look to your Lower Mental Body and your everyday thinking to help get your emotions back to a healthy state. If your mind is struggling with obsession or fear, the realm of the Lower Mental body, look to your Higher Mental Body and your beliefs to soothe your mind. Conversely, if you find yourself overthinking everything, it could be because you are unconsciously trying to keep your emotions from getting the best of you.

THE ETHERIC BODY is connected to your energy level and the Root Chakra. It is the closest body in the layer-cake analogy and the last stop for energy coming into the body. It is also the first to become drained. Think of being the last house on the city water line. Your water pressure is not going to be as strong as the first house on the line. Almost anyone can see the Etheric Body. If you look at someone against a white wall, soften your gaze while looking above his or her head and shoulders; you will most likely see a gray outline about two inches high. This is the person's Etheric Body. If it is less than two inches thick, the person is probably tired or not feeling well. If someone has a gray complexion, this is the Etheric Body actually being pulled into the person's physical body in order to bring in as much energy as possible. This gray coloring on the skin is not a healthy sign, to say the least.

THE EMOTIONAL BODY is frequently out of balance. It is associated with the Sacral Chakra and your emotions. If you are an emotional person, your Emotional Body takes the most energy to maintain balance. When one Outer Body takes more than its share of energy, the bodies below and above it suffer. So when you are very emotional, either super-happy or sad, you may find your energy is low and you have trouble thinking clearly. This is not to say that you should be an emotional zombie, yet being aware of an emotional drain may remind you to take time to eat and sleep while saving important decisions for when you can think clearly. The Emotional Body is what you would think of as your aura. The pretty colors in the aura picture that you get at the psychic fair reflects your emotional status at the time it is taken. Because a person has an emotional blueprint, the main colors will often be the same, yet you will see subtle differences that reveal your emotional state that day. It might be cheating, yet I always take a few breaths, center, and do a little Light Work before I have my Aura picture taken, so it looks nice!

THE LOWER MENTAL BODY reflects your thinking, especially your hopes, fears, and beliefs left over from childhood and views about the world in general. This Outer Body is connected to your Solar Plexus Chakra and mental well-being. Your Lower Mental Body does not focus on your spiritual or higher societal beliefs, yet holds your ideas about how the world will treat you, where you fit in the world, what your parents and society taught you as a child, and how to navigate your daily life. This is another energy-consuming Outer Body. When you obsess or try to think everything out ahead of time, the Lower Mental Body is quickly drained. This leaves you having trouble thinking clearly, discerning, making decisions, and standing up for yourself. A strong Lower Mental Body will have similar strengths as a strong Solar Plexus Chakra. You will not be as susceptible to fear, other people's influence, or societal ideology that doesn't fit your truths. You will find yourself able to think clearly without being affected by unconscious influences, be in control of your emotions, and be able to make decisions by allowing others to offer advice while still honoring your own views.

THE HIGHER MENTAL BODY is communicator of the information perceived from the Intuitive Bodies. This opens up the discussion of distortion. Many think that they are receiving intuitive or psychic information when they are really accessing the Higher Mental Body. This is not to say that the information cannot be accurate, yet this Outer Body tends to be distorted by tribal beliefs as well as social conditions of the day. The Heart Chakra and your higher thoughts are associated with this Outer Body. When you are in need of mental clarity, your Lower Mental Body accesses your higher beliefs to sort out whatever problem it is dealing with. Also, any intuitive information you receive is going to be colored as it passes through your Higher Mental Body. I think this is why people often see angels with wings. Wings have been ingrained in society's mindset, when in fact wings were not associated with angels until about the fourth century. There is no mention of angel wings in the Bible. This misconception is an example of why it is so important to understand the origins of your higher beliefs, and whether they still benefit you.

THE LOWER INTUITIVE BODY is an important one. It is the one that eventually relays the messages from Spirit to the mental bodies. Clarity in this body is important. We all receive guidance from higher sources. If your Outer Bodies are not clear enough the message will be distorted, like a dirty mirror distorts your face. Using the Outer Bodies Meditation will bring more clarity to all of your Outer Bodies. The Lower Intuitive Body is the Outer Body that most psychic information comes from. Associated with your Throat Chakra, your intuition can be clear, yet if your Throat Chakra is weak, you may not trust it enough to act on it. The Lower Intuitive Body is also where the images from the collective unconscious are accessed, as well as daily intuition, guides, and the Akashic Records. That voice, telling you to pay attention, lives here. The vibratory rate is high, yet other vibrations around it can still influence this Outer Body. Often if a psychic is around other psychics, such as at a psychic fair, the strong focus of psychic energy can actually raise the vibration of each psychic allowing all of them to access a greater level of intuition than if he or she was alone. This is also seen in meditation groups; it is easier to meditate and reach out to the Lower Intuitive Body when many people meditate together. If your mind or emotion is out of balance, you may find that your intuitive information does not come through quite as clear.

This is not true of **THE HIGHER INTUITIVE BODY**. The vibration of this Outer Body is at such a high rate that it is difficult to affect it. This type of intuition is sent rather than sought after. Your Lower Intuitive Body does not necessarily access the intuition that comes from the Higher Intuitive Body as much as it does the information sent down from the Transcendent Outer Body into the Higher Intuitive Body and then the Lower Intuitive Body. This is not to say that a psychic cannot access the Higher Intuitive Body, yet it would not necessarily be available at his or her command. The Divine Self might momentarily lift the person to the high vibratory rate of the Higher Intuitive Body, yet a person cannot stay in that energy for more than a split second.

It is even difficult to talk about **THE TRANSCENDENT BODY**. It is vibrating at such a high level, similar to the Higher Intuitive Level, that one cannot perceive it while in his or her physical body. It is thought that this is the Outer Body that someone enters when having a near-death experience or in the actual process of dying.

The main thing to remember about the Outer Bodies is that everything you know, feel, or see is influenced by the clarity of these Outer Bodies. Using the Outer Bodies Meditation will assist you in being as clear and open as possible to receive all the energy and help your guides have to offer.

SOUL SOOTHER

The Outer Bodies Meditation creates a protective yet permeable space around you. As your Outer Bodies strengthen, you become more in tune with your surroundings. You become quickly aware if there is any shift in your energy field, and this allows you to be proactive rather than reactive in your energetic maintenance. Healthy and strong Outer Bodies allow you to remain open and sensitive to those around you. Think of your Outer Bodies as an energetic alarm system. It is important to have your energy open and available as much as possible, and with strong Outer Bodies you can walk — or run — through your hectic day knowing that you are less likely to get surprised by unexpected influences in your environment. You will be aware when you are getting run-down, know when someone is starting to get annoyed, and even know how to distinguish when your child, co-worker, mate, friend, or parent is simply being needy or really needs your help. You can then choose your action based on an informed knowledge of what is really going on instead of making a knee-jerk reaction that pulls you off center and takes you out of the flow of your day. By maintaining a strong and healthy Energetic System, you are at the perfect vibration to be able to fulfill all that your soul has chosen for this lifetime and still accomplish everything on your daily to-do list.

Yet, when your environment is at such a low vibration that it is difficult to maintain your own, using the Light Work - Space Clearing Meditation is perfect to raise your energy to a level that won't allow anything to drag down your own positive vibration.

CHAPTER 20

The Light Work Meditation

*In the daytime there is sunlight and in the
evening there is moonlight and within us there
is clear light that exists beyond to our higher
consciousness. Allow the physical and spiritual
lights to shine together in this moment.*
— *DAVID BENNETT, Voyage of Purpose*

The Light Work – Space Clearing Meditation

1. Take three deep breaths, and with each exhalation, relax your shoulders.
2. Return to breathing normally.
3. Visualize the space you want to clear.
4. Imagine that the entire space is filled with a bright golden light as if there is a million-watt golden bulb, or Divine Being, in the center.
5. See the light reaching every corner and crevice.
6. Envision yourself now standing outside your space, seeing that beautiful, bright light coming out all the windows and doors.
7. Imagine that the intensity and brightness is growing.
8. Ask that only what is for the highest and most loving good for the occupants of the space be allowed to stay and all that is not be removed and sent to the light for healing.

WHERE AND WHEN

I suggest clients use the Light Work - Space Clearing Meditation when there is discord in the house, yet remind them that to clear someone else's space is unethical. This is a highly effective technique for clearing common areas if there is fighting going on in the home, you have a home office, or the house feels stuffy even after you open windows. You do not need to know what the energy is in order to clear it. You can use other colors if you wish, though green, white, and gold work the best. *Platinum or diamond would be overkill.* If you have just bought a house, or piece of furniture, you might want to do this Space Clearing Meditation. Often antiques will hold the energy of the past owners. You may not know who they were, but it is often as if you bring the previous owner home with you. A quick Space Clearing will wipe out the old energy, although if the antique had special significance for the past owner, it might take a few sessions! You can also use this meditation when you have just finished a major cleanup and want to clear away the old energy. For instance, this is a great meditation for after you clean out a closet! I have found that if there is an area of clutter you cannot control, or are having trouble working on, instead of cursing it every time you walk by, bless it and permeate it with golden light. Always ask that any cleansing and clearing be for the highest and most loving good for all concerned.

ETHICS REMINDER: Remember that Light Work can be invasive when used to clean out someone else's space. If you live with children or young adults, you might find that they act out if you do this to their space. It would be as if you came in and literally cleaned it without letting them know. It is better, and more ethical, to teach the other occupants how to do the cleansing or at least ask permission first. If that is not possible, ask your guides to only cleanse what is for the highest and most loving good for the occupants, not what you think they need to have cleaned.

EXAMPLE

Gigi and Kenny are getting ready to sell their house. It has been a happy home but it is time to downsize and they have been offered the perfect opportunity in a new area to start their dream business. Both of them have come to terms with leaving and are excited about their next phase of life. They decide to have friends and family over for a "saying good-bye to the house" party. Everyone cries, sad that Gigi and Kenny are moving out of town. For a few days afterward, Gigi notices feeling sad for no reason. Both Gigi and Kenny are excited about this move and starting the new business, so why is she so sad? She realizes that it must be leftover sad energy from the party. She knows the open house is in a week, so starts doing the Space Clearing Meditation every night before she goes to bed. The day before the open house she realizes that she isn't feeling the blues anymore. The Space Clearing exercise worked! The open house is a success and they get a good offer on their house a week later.

WHY – USING LIGHT WORK

Using Light Work has tangible effects. You may feel like you are pretending, yet just as sounds have vibrations, so do colors. Introducing a color of a higher vibration will shift the energy in a space or a person. This is especially true when the color is combined with intention. Using the information you learned about the associations of the Chakras and Outer Bodies can be a powerful addition to any Light Work. If you know the issue you are dealing with — physical, emotional, mental, or spiritual — you can find the corresponding Chakra or Outer Body that works with that issue. For example, say you are working on fertility. You can work with the Sacral Chakra, associated with the color orange and in charge of the reproductive system, in the Healing Chakra or Space Clear-

SOUL SOOTHERS

ing Meditation. Using the color orange along with the intention of bringing health and vitality to the reproductive system will be more powerful than simply using the color.

Light Work is effective for many of the same reasons that mantras work. Light, via color, has a vibration similar to sound. The vibration affects all it comes in contact with. Often you will find hospital walls with a tinge of blue or green instead of the stark white of forty years ago as these pale colors have been discovered to be soothing. When my sister was picking out colors for the boys' bedroom, I advised her to stay away from deep red, as it is the color of the Root Chakra. The Root Chakra will bring vitality and energy into the room, not what you want for a sleep environment.

The effect of colors on energy also explains why using golden light in the Light Work - Space Clearing Meditation can be so effective. Golden light is filled with the vibration of the Golden Chakra, whose energy is unconditional love. Adding Unconditional Love to any space is like saying to someone, "I am not judging you, I love you no matter what." You are not saying that you condone or will live with whatever that person does, but rather, it's saying that it doesn't change that you still care about them. You can love someone and know you cannot stay with him or her. I recommend the Space Clearing Meditation for people going through a divorce, because often all that angry energy stays in the home. Even if the separation has already taken place, the person who retains the house often stays angry whereas the person who has left the home is able to move on. The leftover energy in the house prolongs the anger. Clearing the energy of the home with the Space Clearing Meditation says to both parties, it is okay to let go and move on. You can both be loved, separately. Prospective buyers can pick up on the leftover discordant energy even if the house is beautiful and well priced. Anytime you sell a home, it is wise to do the

Space Clearing Meditation. It will help the buyers to imagine their energy in the home.

Often parents are tempted to use Light Work to clear out a troubled child's room. It sounds like a great idea, yet to the child it can be very invasive. If you have a daughter who is struggling with privacy and figuring out who she is, and you go into her room, clean out her closets, throw away things you think she doesn't need anymore, and rearrange the floor plan, she is going to freak out! You have invaded her space and tried to define who she is. It is the same with Light Work. Remember, vibrations can be felt. Especially when that vibration is different than the person coming in contact with it. The child, or adult, may not know what you are doing, but the energy will be traceable back to you on an intuitive level, and he or she will resent you without knowing why. That could be worse than the energetic situation you started with!

What can you do? The best thing is to first clear your area, and then any common areas, so that you are in the best energetic surroundings to make clear decisions. Then do the clearing, where you are visualizing yourself outside the house and the million-watt bulb is inside the house shining golden light out of all the windows. Ask that only what is for the highest and most loving good is cleansed and cleared from the entire house in a way that is for the highest and most loving good for all those concerned. Avoid sending the light directly at the person or his or her room. If you want to send light to your brother, don't send it yourself. Imagine yourself in your own pillar of light, and ask his guides to assist him in a way that is for the highest and most loving good of all those concerned. Another technique is to visualize your brother on a soul level, and present him with a silver platter of white light. Put it at his feet and walk away knowing that it is there for him if, on a soul level, he really wants it. If your brother chooses not to take it, it can be sent back to the light to be returned as healing energy for the situation in general. Often the person's soul is able and willing to work with loving energy. You cannot — and should not — force energy on anyone. Trying to force someone to energetically shift will almost always make the situation worse.

The best bet to ensure that you are being as ethical as possible is to always ask that any Light Work you do be for the highest and most loving good of all those concerned as well as intending anything that is unwanted be used instead as healing energy for the situation. Don't forget to ask the Recycling Angels to come and clean up, or intend that what is cleansed and cleared be sent to the light. Otherwise what is cleared from you and the space will build up like an overflowing garbage can.

SOUL SOOTHER

Once you harness the ability to use Light Work in a way that is for the benefit of all those concerned, your soul can start to work to raise your vibration to a level that can connect with your guides and angels with greater ease. Think of your Light Work and resulting higher vibration as scrubbing bubbles for the soul and your surroundings! Your higher vibration will start to positively affect those around you, allowing them to intuitively learn a healthy pattern to emulate or create the environment in which change can happen. You can take control of your own vibration, freeing up your soul, guides, and angels to work with you on the next step in your evolution. You can be a conscious, positive, vibrational force as you go through your daily routine. All of the meditations presented in *Soul Soothers* are designed to allow a deeper connection to your soul, guides, and angels' guidance, while creating a calm and peaceful environment in which you can devote yourself to your spiritual growth without sacrificing your daily responsibilities.

Conclusion

Things in life go best when we lead from the center, in all aspects of life. Keeping our center in this ever rapid time on earth is important and easier than we know. We have moments to center and checking in our day that we normally fill with "Thinking." Like waiting in line, in the car/train, in the shower or the bathroom. Allow yourself to break away from thinking and enter the stillness for a more productive day.

— *DAVID BENNETT, Voyage of Purpose*

By now you have decided which meditations you like best and probably have tried a few during your day. You will find the more you practice these meditations, the quicker and more discreet you can be as you do them. The first time I tried a Walking Meditation, I walked like a toddler. I realized that I had not focused on my feet since I first learned to walk! Now, I can use a Walking Meditation just about anywhere.

You may also have found a certain meditation that you want to spend more time with. There is nothing wrong with putting aside a little time once a day or even once a week to expand any of the *Soul Soother* meditations. Maybe you and a friend could get together for lunch to talk about the lesson in the "Why" section of each chapter and afterward try the corresponding meditation together. You will find that meditating with a group or even another person will strengthen the meditation as well as the benefits.

If you would like to expand any of these meditations, here are a few suggestions. Find a space where you won't be bothered and no one needs your attention. Even though sitting in a car is a good place to meditate, I don't recommend most of the meditations while driving. Turn off your cell phone and, being realistic, decide how long you can spend on a meditation. You might set a kitchen or phone timer and put it under a pillow, or in the back seat of your car. A timer might sound okay when you are listening to it before you meditate, yet after you get into alpha or theta brain wave pattern, its bell will sound like a fire truck siren! Sit comfortably, making sure you have good air circulation and the temperature is not too warm or cold. You will find that expanded meditations will often lower your body temperature and you may get cold. Yet if your space is too warm, you will simply fall asleep. Finally, don't judge your meditation or your mind. Judgment will erase any benefit you are gaining. If you find that the shorter meditations are easier, then it is better to have five short rewarding meditations throughout the day than one longer meditation where you are frustrated and angry with yourself.

EXAMPLE

Here is an example of how a busy woman integrates meditation into her demanding schedule. Tracey has a part-time job at the local middle school as a lunch monitor, an aging mother-in-law who can be demanding, as well as children active in athletics and a husband who travels a lot.

At 6:30 a.m., Tracey opens her eyes and starts to think about her day. Her husband is out of town for work and she has a lot on her plate. Instead of getting tense about how much she has to do, Tracey takes a moment to use the different Blessing Meditations to send loving energy to her husband, home, and the lunchroom she will be monitoring today. She sits at the side of her bed and sinks her roots deep into the ground, breathing in support from Mother Earth, before she patters off to wake the children. Getting them ready and off to school is always a challenge, yet as she makes lunches and in between yelling instructions to the children, she uses the Breathing Meditation, focusing her attention on her breath coming in and leaving her body. She realizes that the children are not listening and so chooses to stop yelling, finishes the sandwiches, and takes a few more deep breaths as she calmly goes upstairs to get them moving along. As she goes into her daughter's room, she takes a second to feel the love she has for her daughter and decides to continue using the Blessing Meditation. She starts by blessing her daughter while finding the missing shoe her daughter is fussing about and then blesses her son as she helps him make his bed. Finally ready, she gets them to the bus stop. Practicing the Activity Meditation, she lets go of any thoughts other than about her children as they wait for the bus. She listens to her daughter's reminder to be picked up at the baseball field and her son telling her that he forgot his science homework on the kitchen table. Tracey tells him she will bring it at lunchtime when she goes to work and continues to give them both her full attention.

As the bus pulls away, Tracey practices the Walking Meditation as she walks back to the house: "Heel-toe, heel-toe." Feeling mindful, she remembers to put her son's homework in her tote bag to bring to work with her. She goes upstairs and gets ready for her shower. She chooses the Chakra Clearing meditation today as she did the Golden Light Meditation yesterday. Imagining each of the rainbow colors coming out of the showerhead, she affirms that she is grounded, ready to connect with people, stand up for herself, be compassionate, communicate her truth, and listen for her higher guidance. She asks the Recycling Angels to come clear up all that has been cleansed and send it to the Light to be returned as healing energy for all she may encounter today. Tracey is now dressed and ready to go to the medical supply store to pick up a new walker for her mother-in-law.

Tracey gets into her car and her "bell" goes off. Because she is in and out of the car so much, she chose the act of getting into her car as her bell. She stops to see where her mind is. She realizes that she is already fretting about seeing her mother-in-law later. She stops and, using the Blessing Meditation, remembers that loving feeling she feels for her daughter and blesses her mother-in-law. Tracey also takes her Bell opportunity to check to make sure she has everything she needs. Now that she has released worrying about her mother-in-law visit, Tracey realizes she forgot her tote bag, which she needs later for work.

Back in the car and driving to the medical supply store, Tracey practices the Activity Meditation and attempts to focus only on driving. It doesn't work well, but she doesn't judge herself, she just laughs and thinks, *At least I tried*! She arrives in the parking lot and knows that getting this walker is going to be a challenge. The store said Medicare won't pay for a new one yet. Her mother-in-law just got a new one, but she doesn't like it and wants the one with bigger wheels. Tracey is up for the fight and starts to walk to the store. Parking is always a hassle here, so she has to park quite far. Doing her Walking Meditation, about halfway to the door she becomes mindful of her stress. She realizes that "fight" isn't the right vibration. She imagines what cooperation would feel like and, using her Attitude Adjuster Meditation, dials herself into a cooperative state of mind. She thinks it over and realizes that it isn't the store's fault. She isn't going to get Medicare to change the rules, and so if she can get them to accept the walker her mother-in-law doesn't like as a trade-in, at least she won't have to pay full price. Why didn't she think of that earlier? Tracey goes in with a big smile, cooperation energy all around her, and walks out with the new walker and an agreement that if she brings the other walker back in good condition, she will only have to pay the difference in price plus a small restocking fee.

As Tracey gets back in the car, her Bell goes off. She checks her mind: it is not on undesirable thoughts, so she checks her body. She realizes that she is sitting cockeyed in the seat. She straightens herself out and drives to the school. Before she gets out of the car, Tracey tries the Twenty-Second Meditation, feeling the weight of her head in her hands; she notices how her mind keeps going on about feeling resentful about spending her morning dealing with the walker. Tracey lets go of that and just allows her head to be totally supported by her hands. Feeling better, she walks into the school, drops off her son's homework, and goes to the lunchroom for her shift. The kids start to file in and, using the Observation Meditation, she watches them as a group. She sees how, for the most part, the boys sit in one group and the girls in the other. In that way, middle-school kids haven't changed much since she went to school. Tracey sees how one child is sitting by himself. He doesn't seem to be dressed like the other kids. She asks another monitor and finds out that he is from another state and just started class last week. She chooses not to do anything about it right now, yet decides that this child will be her topic for her Contemplation Meditation if she gets a chance to do one today. Recalling the love she feels for her daughter, Tracey blesses the child and then blesses the whole lunchroom.

After work, she gets into her car to bring the walker to her mother-in-law. Tracey misses her Bell as she is so focused on thinking of an excuse for not staying long. Her mother-in-law used to be such a fun and happy woman, but ever since she fell and broke her hip, her whole attitude has changed. Tracey wishes she could use the Attitude Adjuster Meditation on someone else! But instead she decides her mother-in-law can wait three minutes and that her Contemplation Meditation is the best way to figure out how to be compassionate with her instead of being resentful. She pulls her little egg-timer out of her tote bag; Tracey never leaves home without it! Setting the timer on the dash, she starts to watch the sand going from the top of the hourglass to the base. She feels her shoulders relax and when thoughts come in, she wipes them aside and returns to watching the sand. She starts to think about her mother-in-law and how much fun she used to be. Tracey thinks about how much pain she was in when her hip broke, and how her son, Tracey's husband, has been traveling so much, he hasn't been able to spend time with his mother, as he usually does.

Tracey regains her compassion, and although she is aware that her mother-in-law is still a difficult woman, she understands why and decides to visit for a few minutes instead of running out the door as soon as she drops off the walker. Tracey gets to the apartment, carrying the walker, and knocks on the door. The door is ajar, so she walks in. Her mother-in-law is on the phone, in a rage. She is giving the what-for to the building superintendent for not fixing the leak in the bathroom. Tracey feels herself getting tense and her compassion going out the window. The leak just happened last night and it's only 2:30! Tracey is exasperated, but quickly recognizes that she is being affected by her mother-in-law's own exasperation at not being in control of her own life. Tracey straightaway goes behind her eyelashes and detaches from her mother-in-law's angry energy. She calms down almost immediately, blesses the poor superintendent, and quietly waits until her mother-in-law gets off the phone. Tracey starts to consciously bring her vibration to a high and loving space, blessing her mother-in-law, realizing that this isn't her issue. The best thing Tracey can do is to be loving to her mother-in-law by listening to her tell her story, yet at the same time reminding her that it has only been a short time, and agreeing that it is difficult when you are not in control of these things. Tracey starts to tell her about her daughter's game today and promises to take some pictures. Demonstrating how to open and close the walker, she stays for another half hour, and then goes to watch her daughter's baseball game. Thank goodness for iPhones and iPads! Tracie can take pictures of her daughter's game and show her mother-in-law the pictures on the iPad.

Back in the car, Tracey is still a little rattled from the visit, so chooses "Release and relax" as her Mantra Meditation phrase. She repeats her mantra for about thirty seconds as she starts up the car. Tracey remembers her Bell: thoughts are great and her body is aligned! The rest of the day goes as usual. She gets to her daughter's game in time to take a few pictures, makes dinner, and finally gets the kids to bed. Tracey is tired, but not as exhausted as she has been in the past when her husband is out of town. Instead of sitting in front of the television, she sits on the sun porch for a few minutes. She realizes that she never sits in this room. It has such a nice energy! Tracey decides to try the Review Meditation; it is not after lunch or before bed, but she has time before her husband calls to say good night.

Tracey goes over the day, discerning if she acted the way she wanted to. She realizes how the meditations help her to shift her energy and make her day run smoother. She repeats her actions with the medical supply company and her mother-in-law just as she did it today, yet when she thinks of the new child at school, she recognizes that she could have spoken to the boy's school counselor or the vice principal to make sure everything was done to introduce the child to his classmates. So she repeats the day in her mind with that change. She will talk to the guidance counselor tomorrow if the boy is still sitting alone. Her husband calls; they chat a little about nothing really, and then she mentions what she learned in her contemplation about the fact that her mother-in-law feels a loss of control and probably misses him coming around with the family. They plan a get-together for them all when he gets back. After hanging up, she gets ready for bed and although she has planned to try the Outer Bodies Meditation before she goes to sleep, she is snoozing by the time she takes her third deep breath.

Tracey is able to add about a half hour of meditation to her day without making many changes. Although you may not add all these meditations into one day, bringing even ten or fifteen minutes of stress reduction and mindfulness into your day will bring results that last long into the future.

Remember not to judge how out of control your mind might be, how little focus you have, or how cranky you may get. Life is an opportunity to celebrate all that is wonderful and to work on your challenges. Using the tools in *Soul Soothers*, you will find your life filled with mindfulness, compassion, and opportunities to be a positive influence to all you come in contact with. Taking control of your energy and your reactions to life offers many benefits besides reducing stress. Your soul will thank you, and so will all of those you come in contact with throughout your busy life.

Endnotes

Why Meditate?

1   Jean Wouters DiMotto, Relaxation, *The American Journal of Nursing* 84, No. 6 (Jun., 1984): 754-758, http://www.jstor.org/stable/3463719.

2   Fadel Zeidan, Susan K. Johnson, David Zhanna, Bruce J. Diamond, and Paula Goolkasian, "Mindfulness Meditation Improves Cognition: Evidence of Brief Mental Training," *Consciousness and Cognition* 19, Issue 2 (June 2010): 597.

Where and When Can I Meditate?

3   Paula Goolkasian, et al., "Mindfulness," 597.

The Breathing Meditations

4   Natural Medicine Talk, http://www.natmedtalk.com/f45/4474-slow-breathing-benefits.html.

5   Mark Matousek, *Is the Way You Breathe Bad for Your Health?* http://www.oprah.com/spirit/Deep-Breathing-Methods-How-Breathing-Reduces-Stress/#ixzz29PuyhQLY.

6   *Living By Design, "Slow Breathing Benefits,"* http://www.livingbydesignonline.com/ananga-living-by-design-blog/2008/3/15/4-reasons-to-tune-into-your-alpha-brainwaves.html.

Bibliography

GOOLKASIAN, PAULA, ET AL. *Mindfulness meditation improves cognition: Evidence of brief mental training. Consciousness & Cognition* 19, no. 2 (June 2010): 597-605. *Academic Search Complete*, EBSCO*host*.

Living By Design. http://www.livingbydesignonline.com/ananga-living-by-design-blog/2008/3/15/4-reasons-to-tune-into-your-alpha-brainwaves.html.

Natural Medicine Talk. "Slow Breathing Benefits." http://www.natmedtalk.com/f45/4474-slow-breathing-benefits.html.

MATOUSEK, MARK. *Is the Way You Breathe Bad for Your Health?*, http://www.oprah.com/spirit/*Deep-Breathing-Methods-How-Breathing-Reduces-Stress/#ixzz29PuyhQLY*.

WOUTERS DIMOTTO, JEAN. *The American Journal of Nursing*, 84, No. 6 (Jun., 1984): 754-755, http://www.jstor.org/stable/3463719.

About the Author

CINDY GRIFFITH-BENNETT, professional intuitive and spiritual counselor and metaphysician has been teaching meditation and spiritual development for over 20 years. She is currently living in Skaneateles NY with her husband, David Bennett with whom she co-authored *Voyage of Purpose*, also published by Findhorn Press. A monthly guest on two local radio stations, Cindy is also a resource on metaphysical matters for television, newspapers and magazines.

She has been able to fulfill her passion for research and learning through her Masters Degree in Consciousness Development by writing her thesis investigating a non religious-specific path to spiritual maturity as presented by mystics from multiple traditions. Find out more about Cindy's work at *PsychicSupport.com*. Cindy tweets daily meditations, tarot numerology and affirmations via @TarotHeals, Facebook at Cindy Griffith's Giving Back Page, Google +, and Pinterest.

Further Findhorn Press Titles

Soul Soothers
Meditation CD

by Cindy Griffith-Bennett

Soul Soothers: Mini Meditations for Busy Lives is designed for those of us that only slow down when stuck in the grocery line! It is a great companion for *Soul Soothers*, the book.

978-1-84409-618-3

Soul Expansion
Meditation CD

by Cindy Griffith-Bennett

These meditations will help the listener gain easier access to their intuition and spiritual guides. They focus on spiritual and psychic growth, and are designed to gradually raise your vibrational levels and awareness.

978-1-84409-619-0

....

Voyage of Purpose
**by D. Bennett &
C. Griffith-Bennett**

David Bennett was caught in a violent storm off the California coast one night where he drowned. While technically "dead," he met beings of light, relived his life, and peeked into his future, which resulted in a complete paradigm shift for him.

978-1-84409-565-0

FINDHORN PRESS

Life-Changing Books

For a complete catalogue,
please contact:

Findhorn Press Ltd
117-121 High Street,
Forres IV36 1AB,
Scotland, UK

t +44 (0)1309 690582
f +44 (0)131 777 2711
e info@findhornpress.com

or consult our catalogue online
(with secure order facility) on
www.findhornpress.com

For information on the Findhorn Foundation:
www.findhorn.org